TRANSACTIONS OF DESIRE, VOLUME II:
ARE YOU ALLERGIC TO THE 21ST CENTURY?

TRANSACTIONS OF DESIRE,
VOLUME II:

ARE

YOU

ALLERGIC

TO

THE

I'll always associate Louise Hay with throwing up garlic-infused vomit. I was on holiday with a friend when I got a bad case of food poisoning, and she prescribed a raw clove whilst hinting that, was I in a better mental state, I wouldn't get sick at all. She then shared with me a dog-eared A4 print-out of Louise Hay's 'Metaphysical Causations' and I was amused to read that my nausea was caused by fear. I was 'Rejecting an idea or experience'. Diarrhoea likewise: 'Fear. Rejection. Running off.' But it was finding the 'probable cause' of AIDS that really made me sick: 'Denial of the self. Sexual guilt. A strong belief in not being "good enough".'

This book contains fifteen responses by artists and writers to the languages of self-help, and to *Safe*, a film directed by Todd Haynes and released twenty years ago, in 1995. In the film, Julianne Moore plays Carol White, a wealthy suburban housewife who becomes increasingly allergic to everyday domestic products and routine activities, eventually moving to an enclosed community in New Mexico. Haynes has spoken about using *Safe* to make a guarded interrogation of his own 'knee-jerk reactions against' such New Age retreats and philosophies, asking why people felt in particular need of such theories and gurus to comprehend their illness, unhappiness or uncertainties.

Set in 1987, at the height of the AIDS epidemic, yet barely directly referencing the disease, the film offers an oblique reflection on the crisis, whilst the ambiguity of Carol's illness – the conflation of the physical and the psychological found in her malaise – and the social relations acted out in the film make it a potent starting point for thinking through structures of patriarchy, social etiquettes, invisible labour, infection, symptom and cure.

Lines of dialogue from the film punctuate and introduce each contribution. A script by Claire Makhlouf Carter sets up a scenario where the social hierarchies of working situations are highlighted, and contextual healing – the placebo – is presented for testing. Laura Morrison likewise focuses on the horrors of medical or institutional control and responds with a variety of anecdotes about living things that have been bred, engineered, evolved or mutated to struggle to live without specialist intervention or dependence, and Camilla Wills describes the silkscreen printing process in relation to the bruise and the permeability of skin and orifices.

The gendered nature of much self-help is responded to by way of Emma Jane Unsworth's short story, a homage to the genre's hopeful emphasis on self-knowledge as a way to find elusive romantic love. Elsewhere Hannah Black reflects upon marriage, property law and slave names via the figure of Mrs White, Louise O'Hare considers the ultimate self-prescription, and feminist biopolitics, and Peter Kingstone reads *Safe* as supernatural thriller whilst mixing social history with recollections of coming out in the late 1980s and 90s.

Todd Haynes has mentioned Louise Hay's book on AIDS in relation to *Safe*, and in this book Chris Paul Daniels has directly engaged with her early writing. The guru's familiar trademark font and verbose encouragements for self-improvement, individual responsibility and love are mixed and converge with the ideological jargon of recent government policy-making, the mantras and bogus affirmations of 'Big Society' and 'right-to-buy'. Jason Wood likewise takes on political rhetoric – the clichéd images of consumer-frenzy-induced debt circulated in the media – to script an ironic parable of individual consumer greed, and provide a sideways critique of the discourse of blame that functions to divert responsibility away from financial institutions and governments for the current economic deficit in the UK.

The textures and surfaces of self-help have diversified – although self-published printed books remain popular, the internet provides ever more ubiquitous tools for self diagnosis, lifestyle instructions and dubious cures. Sarah Perks apes the friendly one-to-one monologues of the genre and their characteristic confusion of symptom and cause with her A–Z of 21ST Century Allergies. Omar Kholeif's solipsistic musings question the use of self-love or masturbation as a preventative measure, suggesting that no procedure will save us from our inadequate corporeality – indeed our mortality; and Sarah M. Harrison considers the physicality of the apparatuses of affluent de-materialised labour – the branded computer goods that pervade certain lifestyles and working situations, and the economic realities they represent – the toxic fumes and wage slaveries behind their production.

Michael Dean's outburst of uncontrollable utterances crops up like a tic or a rash.

'Shockwave', Bridget Penney's text, considers trauma and belief – sites of fallen meteorites as places of pilgrimage, and memories of the 1996 Docklands bombing and contamination warnings from the 1986 Chernobyl fallout.

John Walter is working on 'Alien Sex Club' a large-scale installation (currently touring) which features a maze of graphic imagery, paintings, patterns and audio-visual material interspersed with spaces set up for social interaction or healthcare provision which include a bar, Tarot readings and live HIV testing. Tarot can be seen as pure superstition, or the cards can be understood as a vernacular tool for counselling, instigating moments of free association and conversation. Walter has re-designed the traditional Tarot, and produced a new pack of cards which melds references to pop culture, art history and drug brands related to HIV prevention and transmission. His work for these pages continues in this vein – there is a sense of the Tarot, of latent or ominous meaning in his designs. Drawing on observations from the film – a car number plate, an angry aside – phrases or characters are reiterated and made iconic, standing to offer some different kind of meaning or better fortune to be deciphered.

The ambiguity regarding the cause of Carol White's demise – whether emotional or environmental – might indicate that the health of the vulnerable individual and the society they find themselves in are inextricably linked. If many of the contributions in this book appear concerned with interior – the affective, the function of the institution, and personal histories – it is not caused by a myosis, or even an embrace of the way personal testimony is used as evidence within self-help marketing, but rather it seems to come from an awareness that intimate situations are always inflected by the constructs, the wider politics, that they find themselves within.

—

Louise O'Hare and Sarah Perks, September 2015

The following texts and images were commissioned and edited by Louise O'Hare and Sarah Perks during Summer 2015, to accompany the exhibition *Safe* at HOME, Manchester, 14 November 2015 – 3 January 2016.

This book is the second title in the *Transactions of Desire* series, commissioned by Sarah Perks to explore the manipulative relationships between the emotional, economic, physical, technological, social and political across HOME's inaugural programme.

† Todd Haynes, 'Interview: Todd Haynes by Alison MacLean', *BOMB*, Issue 52, Summer 1995. Available at: http://bombmagazine.org/ article/1874/todd-haynes, last accessed 29 October 2015.

" MRS WHITE? "

MS BLACK

HANNAH BLACK

It is the name which she bears (Juliet, Capulet) that finds itself at war.
JACQUES DERRIDA, 'APHORISM COUNTERTIME', 1986

WHITE

She must have had another name before she married; White is the husband's name that denotes her share in his money and his home.

In the tradition, the wife takes the husband's name. In the tradition, women circulate between men. Exactly because I am not immune to this romance of exchange – exactly because I feel, wrongly, that being taken apart and made new again is not only the promise of violence, but also of love – I say something tough and unromantic: The wife is the property of the husband! But technically, the wife is part of the husband, like the husband's hand or eyebrow or anus, and the wife also shares in the husband's accumulations, like nutrients spread through the bloodstream around a body. Marriage as blood is the law's expectation. Until recently, property law fused husband and wife into one big White two-bodied husband with dominion over everything un-husband-like in his sight: children and animals, servants and slaves.

What is the wife's body, if wife and husband are one, and the husband's name (his father's name) carries the twinned incorporation? Just a dangling remainder, also a seductive incentive, also a machine for producing more husbands and wives. The White bourgeois wife is a historical figure revitalised and kept alive, but ailing, in Carol. She is a title transferred between men.

A woman is made up not of her physical body, which is decorative or embarrassing because faintly pointless, but of a social relation between men. This problematic abstract-ness of women gets concretised as body anxiety, representational freak-outs, gender essentialist panics, and misogynist accusations of inauthenticity and vanity. I've been there. When Mrs White's physical being asserts itself, it manifests as a genderless stream of distress signals: a nosebleed, vomit, a swollen tongue.

For many feminists in Europe and European settler colonies, the wife, rather than the servant or the slave, came to serve as the metonym for patriarchal domination. There is no good reason for that. Women are everywhere, aphoristic, a cut in the world, but the racialised woman gets drowned in the category of her race, analytically speaking.

The White wife cries crocodile tears for the Black slave, who she deploys merely as an analogy. The comparison is, interestingly, not possible in reverse. The bourgeois wife says, 'Don't treat me like your slave!' But the slave doesn't say, 'Don't treat me like your wife!' The husband transfers his social standing to the wife; the master doesn't imbue the slave with his. The husband can't strike a deal with the wife because the wife is himself; he can't strike a deal with the slave because the slave is no one. The White wife, because she is owned, also owns herself: Mr White is the crown of her self-ownership, which she develops defiantly, sometimes against him. The Black slave, because she is owned, owns nothing.

R told me she dreamed of a White couple merging into one body, which then became, in a dream scene change, the swinging naked figure in Rihanna's 'BBHMM' video. How did you feel about the body in front of you, R? *Desire, anger and pity.*

Even leeched of reproductive power, the sex between the Whites is still functional. Its function is to uphold the integrity of the White household. To check out of this sexual contract without breaking it, you have to call in sick. Yes, the usual commonplaces of critique: the accusation that the White heterosexual matrix is subordinated to function, always already instrumental, a technology of violence. But where its outside is understood as the inside's undoing or opposition, it also becomes its instrument. The child, the queer, the servant and even now still the slave in her long afterlife make up the material of the White wife, through incorporation or negative affirmation.

BLACK

Sometimes people wince when I say my name and sometimes they smile or make a joke. I got it from my mother, but it doesn't belong to her either, and it doesn't describe her. She didn't get it from where her people come from: the vague, drab eastern villages where the Russians sent their Jews, that whole threadbare and indigestible history.

The story of the origin of this name is purely bureaucratic. A clerk, finding no trace of a surname among the illiterate migrants in front of him, scrawled Black on a form. That was four generations ago. It only takes two generations for a name to become institutional, through either patriarchal or matriarchal transmission.

But I was given my father's name at birth. This is a Scottish name, common in Jamaica, inherited from a plantation owner. Even more emphatically than a marital name, it expresses a property relation, not an origin. Frederick Douglass wrote, 'Slavery does away with fathers.' It does so in favour of a Black matriarchal transmission under constant attack, and in favour of the master, who takes the place of the father. The slave does not become infused with the master's power. I did away with my father's name, though it still remains on my passport, my bank account, my documents.

My father's friends used the term 'slave names', the names that they gave up and replaced with African or Arabic names. The slave name, like the bureaucratic invention, can become institutionalised as family through generations, but it carries the institution's violence within it. My father kept his slave name, perhaps out of sentimental attachment to his own father, perhaps just because it was easier.

My White mother, Ms Black, appended her name to my name, another imposed name: but all names are impositions of one kind or another. She explained, 'People look at me strangely when they see we have different names.' I think in fact they looked at her strangely for another reason. I was pained and embarrassed by my new name and also by the constant invocations of the history of slavery in my father's household. I privately mocked those who changed their names to sound more African. I lived in my own name like someone might stop for a moment underneath an anonymous bus shelter in a brief squall of rain. I had to be called something, but it didn't matter what. 'The inhumanity or the ahumanity of the name.' What does a name name? Endless reversions.

Educated by, in and for White people, my portion of the general blackness was instrumentalised to serve a fantasy of inclusion. I chose a hedgehog strategy, hoping to make myself indigestible; I wore my hair like a public humiliation. At school and in my mother's house, I fought to be something other than a symbol of White pride in Black assimilation: the latter is the mulatta's permanent fate, if she isn't careful. In my father's house, I was overwhelmed by shame, a kind of relief. 'If you want to *be* somebody, you have to be what doesn't meet the eye.' A name, that unreal appendage? The mulatta hides herself inside herself, just like race vanishes every time it appears, just like race appears in its vanishing. It slips through the spaces between the words. It rubs at the corners of the frame.

BLACK & WHITE

The couple were cleaved, was cleaved, by irreconcilable differences. When Juliet first met Romeo, she was irritated on sight: his almond eyes behind expensive glasses, his mouth positioned in a blurry pout that nevertheless produced the most precise sentences. Within 24 hours she was in love with him, for the same reasons. They lay in bed examining each other's eyes: 'Your eyes are the same as mine!' It was a miracle, obviously. In retrospect, this time is like a muted video: the picture moves, it looks good, but you don't understand what is being expressed. Juliet looks in her diary to try to remember, but under the first relevant date, 21 August 2011, it just says 'Romeo', and after that, almost a month later: 'I wish I wrote more when I was happy, so I could remember, but at the time I don't want to believe that I will ever forget.'

Juliet, a Londoner, is away during the riots in London, during the mass mourning, during the Black uprising. She is with Romeo. He asks her where her family come from. Mulatta histories always take a long time to tell. He isn't listening. 'You could be from anywhere,' he says. She accuses him of only really loving White women. 'I love beauty,' he says vaguely. *Beauty is white supremacist*, she thinks but doesn't say. Romeo falls in love with Mrs White, but Mrs White won't leave her husband. Juliet is astonished: wouldn't Romeo prefer death with Juliet to a long life in the suburbs? There are pages and pages in the diary, months and months, of her trying to make herself believe that he doesn't love her. Her loving effort in trying to believe he doesn't love her becomes part of the situation of their continuing, broken love. Romeo loved Mrs White pragmatically, presciently, but he would only ever love Juliet in the past tense. She was always loving him in the present and future, but he would only love her once the time he could have loved her was over. Then he would write to her and say, punctually delayed, 'I used to love you.' And then, right on cue, too early, she would fall in love with him again. Pages and pages where, in order to believe that Romeo doesn't love her, Juliet, crazy with love, writes detailed descriptions of the sex she imagines he is having with Mrs White, who at this point has finally left her husband for him.

'Love is bourgeois,' said Romeo, who considered himself, with deliberate irony, a bourgeois, and later, 'Juliet, you are the least bourgeois person I know.' Juliet loves Romeo partly because, like her, he is *of colour*, but since he met Mrs White, Romeo says he defines as White, is basically White, might as well be White. What does it mean to claim whiteness when whiteness doesn't claim you? Contemplating this impasse, Juliet feels language curdling in her brain. The feeling of being struck dumb is interesting to her, because she is always talking. She writes to herself, very sternly: 'I want him to release me from the obligations of my desire, but I know it's not possible, because only I can do that for myself.' No, Juliet, not even you...

They don't know how to talk to each other; they only know how to argue and have sex. She sees him after a two-month break and he crosses the crowded bar and stands near her and she is shaking with excitement and fear and she says to him, 'Stand further away, you have to stand further away, I'm shaking,' and he says, 'I don't want to, I can't.' Then she goes home, still shaking, and writes in her diary, a message to her future self: 'I love him, I don't care about your tears.' 27 June: 'I can't see through this darkness, dark fog…' In a dream, in a burned house, they translate a passage in a book together, and he presses against her, so that she feels, with a wave of overwhelming love, his hard dick. She wakes up crying. Later, she discovers that she had the dream on the same night that Mrs White left him.

He cries for Mrs White in Juliet's arms. Later, Mrs White comes back. Romeo thinks Juliet looks Semitic, like her mother, and that in America no one will think she looks Black. She is upset but says nothing. She goes to America and writes: 'He is 3500 miles away, he can't hurt me any more.' Later she wonders if her motive for going to America was just to be able to write that sentence. She returns from America after a year, triumphantly Black. Mrs White and Romeo have broken up. They have sex one last time. She loves him so much, she will never love anyone like that again, she thinks, because it was so dumbly pure, pure longing. He holds her and says he loves her. Juliet, I love you, Juliet. The words feel full. They start arguing about race and they don't stop. Her blackness, delayed by desire, finally appears between them, a geopolitical insertion. Without Ferguson and after, without the quelled summer riots in London, without the 'migrant crisis', perhaps she would not have bothered to insist. She wants a name. She no longer wants to die of him, in him.

She tries to take him with her. She cites his father, who, like hers, is not White, but he loves his mother, who, like hers, is. She tries to leave him. Still the magnetism, the strange magic of living in different times, at the same time, holds her in the terrible blankness of his love, his lack of love, his love, etc. 'I will love him and hate him forever.' Several variations on this simple point. She understands at last that she has to do something unforgiveable, to break the cyclical time of their love/non-love. She screams and cries; she offends his sensibilities. 'You're crazy,' he says, beautiful eyes half-closed. They look at each other with hatred. 'My love for you is like the soft place on a baby's head,' she weeps, hysterical, furious, in love, 'it never closes.' She sees a White husband surface in his not-White face. She understands at last that he loved Mrs White more than he loved her. His name is not really Romeo, and hers is not really Juliet.

"

**WE CAN TURN IT ON AND
OFF LIKE A SWITCH, WE JUST
DON'T KNOW HOW TO MAKE
IT GO AWAY.**

"

LIFE LESSONS
FROM A TINY TREE

LAURA MORRISON

Under normal circumstances, and for as long as she can remember,
Laura has been chronically unable to detach a tale from its telling.
The feeling that characters and worlds on screen are real and
intolerably present – whether hammily acted, badly produced or
banal – has amounted to a lamentable over-sensitivity to stories
(especially films), and eventually, to a great hole in her cultural
knowledge that she struggles to hide.

Peter and the Wolf
The NeverEnding Story
The X Files
Apollo 13
Melancholia

Now she looks away during conversations about movies and as if
in her own, more pressing thoughts, she stares, captivated by a
piece of fluff or a shape in the clouds: another dimension of signifi-
cance visible only to her. Or, in a state of irresistible animation – careful
however, to preserve the volatility needed to phase back out – she
skillfully diverts the conversation.

The commission to use a film that she had never seen as a prompt for new artwork released Laura temporarily and for the first time in a long time she watched with ease. Paying special attention to the set-design and dramaturgy, she played back a scene from the middle of the film – the spine, she thought – with interest. In the room are an allergy specialist, a nurse and the patient: male / white in a white lab coat and sterile gloves; female / black in a white lab coat and sterile gloves; female / white in a pale blue gown with bare arms. Carol is injected with around fifty different food and mould tinctures to determine her 'neutralisation dose'. Nothing happens for a while. It's a bit boring and suspense builds. Then she has a strong reaction. The clinician assesses her state:

We have palpitations and deep distress, in conjunction with a racing pulse rate of 104. There's flushing and some wheezing. We have swelling in the mouth. This is a big one Carol... milk's a biggie!

Neutralised and recovering, the man tells her:

We can turn it on and off like a switch, we just don't know how to make it go away...

'It was more like a high-end 90s kitchen or alien autopsy room! The actors had this extreme gravitation. The doctor and nurse in orbit and Carol like a star on the brink. Maybe I should have talked to my astrology friend about it... Leaving Carol on her own like that to wait for a reaction, and the way the nurse was rummaging behind the worktop with her back popping up... totally celestial.'

Incidentally, Laura recently learned that in front of a black hole with your feet closest to it and your head furthest away, the variation in gravitational force pulling you in would be that much greater at your feet than at your head so as to tear your whole body apart. She finds it disappointing somehow that you would be destroyed before entering the place nothing ever comes back from. Being told this by the man you love is bliss, she had thought. 'Nothing ever comes out. Nothing,' he had said.

The surgery scene opens with a bird's-eye view of the work surface. The shot rotates slowly from left to right, past needles, a gloved hand completing a chart, trays of vials with silver caps, and stops above two further gloved hands injecting the patient's arm. It hovers over a grid of red-raw blotches labelled on the skin in blue pen as: ABCD across and 12345 down. There are patches under the clinician's white gloves indicating moisture. He quivers with the control required to inject D1. As he pulls the needle, a tiny ball of blood emerges and the scene cuts. Laura wonders if the arm was a stunt double or if Julianne Moore did it.

Dr Reynolds, the allergy specialist, is the most reassuring chacacter in the film. Laura likes his medium-deep voice and the way he handles Carol: the softness of touch she imagines from his tight, sterile gloves on her freckly upper arm. He reminds her of a used car salesman, or the father of an old school-friend, who seemed inexplicably relaxed with the ordeal of teenage children. He addresses Carol:

So most of the time there's a trigger: new carpeting, new kitchen, new car, somebody who works around paint fumes or strong fragrances. Then one day, Bam! It hits you, and your body is reacting to everything like a Geiger counter.

Despite the diversion provided by the art commission, when Carol reacts to the dose of milk, her troubled breathing is hard for Laura to watch. Instead of pausing the film or turning it off, she takes comfort in imagining the actors and crew resisting laughter as Carol loses control. She remembers being alarmed but sympathetic to a driver's deeply ingrained tick on a coach to Stansted airport years earlier:

'A few times a minute he would crane his head to the side in a kind of convulsion. His eyes were off the road. It wasn't voluntary or involuntary.'

She thinks perhaps it's an understandable reaction to the absurdity of being responsible for fifty human lives in proximity to large, heavy objects moving at great speed, for hours at a time. She feels sorry for him and she feels her own weakness.

Laura likes calm, compact men: dense, with extreme mental facility, especially for maths, physics, the universe; men she is able to fight fairly, with dignity, whose clothes could be shared but who in the end would overpower her due to the natural fibres of their muscles. The more they happen to be kind, or inexperienced in her ways, the more they play along when she tries to measure herself against them. They may take care even, that she doesn't hurt *herself*.

Last summer, Laura went to a barbeque in Brooklyn with the only person she could feel anything for, after the most crushing and understandable of slow departures the winter previous – and met Liz.

Liz was a PhD candidate at Cornell, writing on the relationship between pleasure and coercion. 'Tell me what you mean!?' she said to Liz, and the most interesting and awful hypothesis was briefly explained to her. With her usual energy on these occasions, Laura told Liz about her work with Beatrice, an artist from London who would be coming to New York soon, and suggested they visit Liz in Ithaca, at Cornell – that it could be significant to all three.

The car rental company made a mistake and no basic vehicles were available, so the following week, at no extra cost, Laura and Beatrice drove to Ithaca in a burgundy Chevrolet Silverado pick-up truck.

They swam at Buttermilk Falls, where the glacial water calmed the naval piercing of one and made her glow, and encouraged the vanity of the other. The only other thin people and real swimmers present were a sinewy couple whose health masked their agedness. They watched Laura swim seriously with what seemed to her a well-disguised relief – as if one of their own had been returned – but they were humble people. Their approval felt ancient and nourishing and Laura happily watched Beatrice read on the grass each time she turned her back on two plump boys standing in the shallows. The tie-dye she had worn on their first meeting – when they had both made their demands – fell off her shoulder in the late afternoon sun and her hair was wet.

James, Liz's friend, was with her in the driveway grilling corn and vegetarian hotdogs when the girls pulled up, joking awkwardly about 'the pussy wagon… the shame-mobile.' His English Bulldog, 'Mack', rearranged himself around the feet of his camping seat and snorted with the effort of lying down again. Without looking up, and addressing only the animal, James said, 'Yes, they did this to you… made you look the way you do and be bad at breathing.' Laura, on guard, suspected he could have talked like that for a long time. She felt bad, but was he self-conscious? After a pause there was a more normal introduction, with eye contact and the shaking of hands.

James explained that Mack would have health complications, as Bulldogs most inevitably do, and the veterinary bills would 'necessitate killing him off'. He mentioned some duties: cleaning the folds in Mack's face every couple of days to avoid yeast infections; using his finger to dislodge faeces, relieving the dog. The animals were bred by British colonialists for bull-baiting (fights to the death). They are prone to disease with a uselessly undershot jaw, for the original purpose of clamping down and hanging on till the end. They have a skull so large as to necessitate pre-planned canine caesarean-section. James wasn't a 'fancier' preserving the stock. No. Mack had been abandoned then adopted by James and friends, with the dissonant sentiment that since he was alive, and as long as some balance existed between his health and their finances, he might live out his days.

There were less than twenty-four hours to spend in Ithaca. Before leaving, they went to swim at Cayuga, one of New York's longest glacial finger-lakes. They found James and Mack already on the rocks, in the sun, Mack wandering around the edge with flustered intention. Seemingly without pain, he walloped himself along, poorly adjusted as he was to the relationship between his paws, body-weight, the crevices and uneven ground. James kept a constant eye. He calmly rescued the dog each time Mack tried to swim out, and giving up after a metre or two, began a wide U-turn. Facing the rocks once more, with James' arm supporting his belly, Mack swam violently, chin desperately elevated, scratching unknowingly, with absolute indignity, back to the rocks.

Every Tuesday in Brooklyn, the Botanic Garden waives the $12 entry fee. Beatrice went on a Wednesday as her stay was short. There, beside the Capsicums, Water Lilies, Weeping Hemlocks and English Yews, is the C. V. Starr Bonsai Museum.

'There is no bonsai "tree" per se,' Julian, the collection's curator explains.

These are normal trees that would have grown to twenty or thirty feet. In the shallow bed of their pots, the bonsai develop capillary systems of absorbent roots that thrive in the fine, often loose or rocky soil. Under these conditions, with pruning and care, come the mature, if miniature, trees. They think their root system is huge, that they must be a 30 foot tree living in the landscape; with ideal growing conditions.

Very rarely is a bonsai given a name, but the Juniper that stands ceremonially outside the entrance is named 'Fudo'. Fudo is considered one of the top five Juniper bonsai in Japanese history and is so called because of the strong aura it projected when alive, and even now in death. The shape of Fudo's natural dead wood resembles the flaming nimbus of the Buddhist deity *Fudo-myoo*: the immovable protector, said to protect the living by burning away all impediments.

Beatrice told Laura about the tree and she visited it several times once she was on her own again. It was first seen by Botanic Garden representatives in November 1969 when a tour-group of garden members visited the Murata Nursery while in Japan. After admiring many of the trees available for purchase, two members of the group kept wandering back to look at a gnarled and twisted 'old timer'. To see it was to read at a glance its autobiography; lonely centuries of frugal existence in an out-of-the-way mountainous region somewhere in Japan, buffeted by continuous winds and winter storms, but always with the strength to survive. Telephone calls and letters expressed interest in the acquisition of the tree for the Botanic Garden. Mr Murata was noncommittal but eventually the communication came:

Personally, I do wish to keep this fine tree in my private collection as long as I live; but since I am in the trade, I am willing to sell it only if some vital qualifications are met. Recently, air pollution in Japan is becoming unbearable for both human beings and especially for trees in the garden. I am not against progress, but trees do not understand it. They just have to suffer and sometimes die quietly. I have been told that Brooklyn Botanic Garden is large enough that it cannot possibly have a pollution problem within its premises. There is no place in America like the Brooklyn Botanic Garden where all necessary facilities are available for proper care. Above all, it is highly important that American people, most of whom are still relatively strange to our fine art of bonsai, will have a chance to appreciate the tree. I have said to my friends that I would not sell it even for a million dollars, if the Brooklyn Botanic Garden were a commercial nursery; but I know BBG staff would love and care for my tree, not just professionally, but wholeheartedly. Anyway, it is all right now and I feel as if I am giving my own daughter to an American to be married.

Fudo arrived in New York via Pan American Airways and was officially met at Kennedy International Airport by Robert S. Tomson, Assistant Director of the Botanic Gardens, together with representatives of the US Department of Agriculture. The prescribed fumigation treatment was carried out, and Fudo was put on display in a screened quarantine cage, still damp from her insecticidal bath. In October 1971, a year after it arrived, Fudo was declared dead without ever having become acclimated to the new home, despite extraordinarily special care. Her ancient body was said to be around eight-hundred and fifty years of age.

"

I'VE JUST BEEN A LITTLE ... UNDER THE WEATHER.

"

SHOCKWAVE

BRIDGET PENNEY

In my dream, crowds were heading towards the National Gallery to collect the colour plates for their copies of the new book on the Van Gogh exhibition. The gallery, Trafalgar Square and the streets leading on to it were chock-a-block. Suddenly there was a huge explosion in the sky overhead. Objects streamed down killing or injuring everyone in the crowd. Dust rose from fresh craters in the pavement; a yellow haze with the sharp smell of mustard suffocated those who were still trying to run away.

Somehow I passed from being one of the crowd to watching it on the news. There wasn't much to see, just remotely relayed CCTV footage of the first objects hitting the gallery roof and people's faces, upturned, like they had an idea something might be coming. No one could make out what was happening, we just knew it was really bad. 'Watch the skies!' *Then* the screen goes black.

Ever since I read that dreamers don't experience surprise, I've tried to evaluate my reaction to strange things which happen in my dreams. The loudness of the National Gallery explosion, the vividness of its vibration, impact and dust shocked, as distinct from surprised, me. Lying awake the next morning I considered the possibility that it had piggy-backed on a memory I already had, of turning the key in my front door at the instant the Canary Wharf bomb went off. I have absolutely no idea of what I was doing on either side of that moment, but the intense emotions of those few seconds, shock, dread and selfish relief – that although I was close enough to hear the explosion, I wasn't affected and those I cared most intimately about were all accounted for – are permanently locked away out of sequential time.

The day after my dream, 15 February 2013, the news carried a story about a meteorite exploding in the sky above the Urals, narrowly missing the city of Chelyabinsk. This explosion took place at 9:20 YEKT, 4:20 GMT. Had the sound of the meteorite's disintegration coincided with the explosion in my dream? I didn't seen how that could be, though in a few days' time, if the wind continued from the east, we might possibly breathe in traces of meteorite dust or experience its haze over the low winter sun. When the same wind carried radioactive fallout from Chernobyl in 1986, there were public health warnings against going out in the rain, or at least making sure you had an umbrella to minimise possible contamination. I was walking west along a beach one sunny spring afternoon without even a coat when the heavens opened. Somehow, though it really wasn't funny, my reaction was to laugh and stretch out my arms. Perhaps it was a strange kind of guilt at the minimal risk we were exposed to, compared with the awful fate of the people who had already died. Or an example of black humour as an effective coping strategy. An instance of this that I use on a weekly basis: I really hate shopping malls, so whenever I enter one I think about the mall scenes in *Dawn of the Dead* and become one of the people who were happy there.

Statistics about the Chelyabinsk meteor quickly emerged. Originally a small near-Earth asteroid, it became a brilliant superbolide meteor entering the atmosphere above Russia, described as brighter than the sun from 100 kilometres away and casting moving shadows as it travelled at a speed of 19.16 plus or minus 0.15 kilometres per second. With its diameter estimated at around 20 metres and an estimated initial mass of about 10,000 tonnes (heavier than the Eiffel Tower), it became the largest object to enter the Earth's atmosphere since the 1908 Tunguska event which devastated 2000 square kilometres of Siberian forest, knocking over an estimated 80 million trees. The Chelyabinsk meteor exploded about 29.7 kilometres above the earth. The bulk of the object's energy was absorbed by the atmosphere, with a total kinetic energy before atmospheric impact equivalent to approximately 500 kilotonnes of TNT. That's twenty to thirty times more energy than was released by the atomic bomb detonated at Hiroshima or about the same as a thermonuclear W88 warhead carried by the Trident II missile.

The infrasonic shockwave resulting from the explosion of the Chelyabinsk meteor was picked up by twenty listening posts in the Comprehensive Nuclear Test Ban Treaty Organisation network; the furthest afield 14,450 kilometres away in Antarctica. In fact the shockwave travelled some 85,000 kilometres, circling the Earth twice in three days at a speed of around 340 metres per second. It was the loudest sound ever recorded, yet at a frequency too low for humans to hear.

Viewing footage culled from CCTV that morning in Chelyabinsk, it's evident that this is true. When windows shatter into a room, sending curtains and blinds arcing up, most people's reaction is bewilderment rather than panic. Schoolchildren rush to the broken windows of their classroom; one girl puts her hands over her ears but it's to shut out the continuing noise of glass disintegrating and the alarms going off in buildings all around. An old factory building, caught by a security camera across its yard, all but disappears in the incandescent flash of the meteor's passage, rematerialising with only half the windows on its eight storeys intact. People in the streets spoke of feeling the meteor's heat as it passed overhead. They reported smelling gunpowder, sulphur and 'burning odours' from around an hour after the atmospheric impact and for the rest of the day. On a motorway outside Chelyabinsk, a dashcam records the shallow, sloping trajectory of the meteor as it bursts into light. Lorries, black tarmac, deep snow and power lines are momentarily erased as it seems like the sun has come to earth.

Defence early warning systems, looking for threats of terrestrial origin, only scan a narrow angle above the horizon and are unlikely to detect an object falling from space. Yet scientists from all over the world had been paying close attention to the sky because a larger asteroid which had been flagged as a potential danger was expected to pass close by the earth that day. 'Duende', as it was named, eventually passed 27,743 kilometres above the Earth's surface at 19:25 GMT, fifteen hours after the Chelyabinsk meteor's spectacular atmospheric impact. Deterrent strategies had included a vague, possibly jokey mention of reflective paint – could the whole earth, or even a significant part of it, really be camouflaged into a gigantic mirrorball? Or could a missile be fired to bounce the meteorite away onto a harmless trajectory or alternatively shatter it into smithereens too small to be pulled down by Earth's gravitational field? Claims that a Russian missile had caused the Chelyabinsk meteor to break up in the atmosphere, thereby averting disaster, appeared spurious. Indeed this relatively small extrater-restrial rock seemed to have gone completely under the radar. Its detonation, causing a shockwave that damaged 7200 properties across six cities and injured 1500 people with flying glass – fortunately no fatalities – was literally as a bolt from the blue.

The Russian government announced that it would pay to replace all the windows broken by the shockwave but not for the glassed-in balconies that front so many flats and provide some respite from the harsh winter climate and a place to dry clothes without them freezing solid. In Chelyabinsk in February, the temperature can drop to -18°c. The regional emergency ministry asked people not to panic and advised them to help keep themselves warm by securing their broken windows with plywood and plastic. Glaziers would have to work around the clock for months to reglaze all those broken panes. Of more immediate concern may have been that supplies of plywood and plastic sheeting must have quickly run out. Yet more footage on YouTube is from a camera suddenly switched on to follow the shockwave, its owner running out onto the balcony to film through an aperture shaped by the edge of a broken pane. Later they would have had to fill that hole with whatever materials came to hand. Spiderwebs of tape holding cardboard and carrier bags in place, anything to keep the intense cold at bay.

The fate of the Chelyabinsk meteor quickly became a matter for different kinds of speculation. After the spectacular 'air burst', its fragments entered dark flight (no longer emitting light) and created a strewn field of numerous meteorites on the snowy ground. At Lake Chebarkul, about 60 kilometres from Chelyabinsk, local fisherman saw the meteor disintegrate into seven pieces with one falling on the shore opposite Chebarkul town 'whipping up a pillar of ice, water and steam' and forming 'a giant circular ice hole 8 metres in diameter' according to the police report. Police immediately cordoned off the area but couldn't stop scientists and other interested people flocking to the lake. Government warnings for people to stay away from meteorite fragments were equally ignored. Video footage of trees blazing above snow-covered valleys were said to show other potential impact sites. Something of a meteorite 'rush' was underway. Or, as RT.com put it: 'A number of local opportunists began selling alleged pieces of the space rock in a bid to make a quick fortune.' One classified ad in the jewellery section of Russian website Avito offered, with suspicious promptness, 'Two vans of the Chelyabinsk meteorite. Price can be negotiated.'

Tiny black fragments of rock, gathered from around the hole in the lake, were found to contain about 10% iron. The Chelyabinsk meteorite was confirmed to be an 'ordinary chondrite' belonging to by far the most common group of space rocks found on Earth. One listed on eBay in June 2013 was described as an 'Astonishing beauty direct from Russia' and stated: 'Welcome, Dear Guests! / You are bidding on an Astonishing piece of / Meteorite that fell in / Russia's City of Chelyabinsk on February 15, 2013. This Unique piece would satisfy the Hunger of / Interest both for Scientists and Private Collectors.' At this point lumps of up to half-a-kilo in weight were on offer at a price roughly ten times that of silver. Naturally, buyers were encouraged to be wary and make sure for their money they were getting an authentic bit of the 'celestial body': 'Every Meteorite that we sell comes with a Disc, that contains Photos and Video Footage of LIVE Discovering Process!'

At the start of September 2013, divers in Lake Cherbarkul located a large fragment of rock covered by silt and mud on the lakebed, but it was not until 16 October, only a month before the lake would freeze again for the winter, that they were able to bring to shore 'the largest-discovered fragment of a Russian meteorite, weighing around 570 kilograms... The huge meteorite chunk split into three pieces when scientists tried to weigh it. The precise weight could not be established because the heavy object broke the scales.' Footage of the divers struggling to lift the rock out of the lake brings home how extremely dense this 'ordinary chondrite meteorite' is. An appreciative group of watchers have cameras trained on their every move.

Meanwhile, on 17 September 2013, LifeNews.ru reported that the Church of the Chelyabinsk Meteorite, founded by 'paranormalist' Andrey Breyvichko, 'are busy holding rites on the shores of the lake, trying to protect the meteorite by building "protective barriers" around it'. Breyvichko claimed the rock contains 'a set of moral and legal norms that will help people live at a new stage of spiritual knowledge development'. He was strongly opposed to the attempts to lift the chunk out of the lake, claiming that as long as the meteorite stays at the bottom of the lake, it was 'in a positive environment'. The stakes were high. Breyvichko also described the meteor as powerful enough to trigger the Apocalypse. In mid-September 2013 he told the first Regional Channel, 'Contact with outsiders, who treat it as an average stone, can violate the information contained in it. We already see the perturbation of the noosphere from constant attempts to lift the meteorite in fomenting international instability around Syria.'

The fifty 'psychic priests' of the Church of the Chelyabinsk Meteorite regarded the data stored inside the meteorite as the 'testimonies'. They wanted the local authorities to give them the rock, for which they planned to build a temple in Chelyabinsk. 'I think it won't hurt Chelyabinsk to become a truly holy city, home to a great temple that will be the object of pilgrimage for millions of people from across the world,' Breyvichko stated. The 570 kilograms fragment retrieved from the bed of Lake Cherbakul is now displayed, with extensive supporting and interpretive material,

in the natural history section of Chelyabinsk Regional Museum.
Smaller pieces of the Chelyabinsk meteorite continue to circulate.
In September 2015, a 'really nice cute rare Chelyabinsk ordinary
chondrite meteorite that fell Feb. 15, 2013 at 9:21 AM (local time)
in the Chelyabinskaya Oblast Region of Russia' approximately
33 × 33 millimetres and weighing 1.6 grams is offered for £28.67
plus shipping from Colorado. It's described as having 'a nice fusion
crust.' The seller also remarks that, 'Smaller size Chelyabinsk
meteorites are even more rare than larger size.' This tiny meteorite
comes with a 'collector magnet' that the buyer can stick to their
fridge. It shows three views of the meteor's passage. What looks
like a blazing sun on a pin unzips the sky above tall leafless trees.
Next to it a calmer image of white smoke demonstrates a sloping
trajectory of around 45°. The largest of the three views shows a
low, fiery, cloudy halo above trees, snow and possibly a frozen
lake. Quite a talking point on the fridge and a useful mnemonic
so the buyer can remember what meteorites, in the words of the
seller, are all about.

'Meteorites originate in outer space from the heads of comets
from the asteroid belt from the Moon, Mars and beyond and are
recognized as a gift from another world.

Meteorites will help you expand your metaphysical awareness
and help connect you with energies from other planets.'

"

YOU KNOW CAROL, YOU DO NOT SWEAT.

"

THE FORCE OF MEANING ----------------

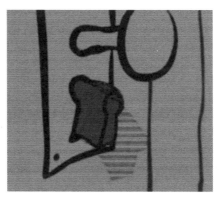

-------------------------------------- CORRESPONDS TO RISK

SECOND THOUGHTS

I am convinced by people who can be inventive at their openings. Because connection with the world comes through the orifices. I want the silkscreen process to perform in its flatness and enact something like this. That is, the permeability of the body and a strong compulsion for contact. The bitmap is atomised. The screen is made up of holes. Through which fluid information is pushed, for diffusion and new meaning. The inks and chemicals are oil and water-based (a bit like gel pharmaceuticals). So the process becomes a conundrum of what is solvent, and what is fast, insoluble. Or what parts flow and what remains unaccountable. But meaning rests in both zones. During exposure the image appears on the screen like a ghost walking through a wall. Reaffirming faith in the void. And over-exposure is burn out. That's clear from normal life too. I feel self-conscious, kind of lamentable, each time I use the high-pressure hose to rinse a screen, sometimes more than thirty times a day – compared to something like prodigious when using spray paint. The screen-printed surface (paper, plastic, fabric) accepts the effects of compression and stress in a play of bruising. Every movement is directed downwards, to the depth of the earth. A crime scene – where there's a chance that the formless can be presented as discourse. You bury the victim, but at the same time sow and harvest. In the act of printing, the vacated mark of the artist's body is variously apparent depending on the strength of contact. Most of the prints are life-size. *Find your exit.*

"
DO YOU SMELL FUMES?

"

DEMO SAFE
CLAIRE MAKHLOUF CARTER
13 NOVEMBER 2015
HOME MANCHESTER

PRE-EVENT VERSION 04
© 21 / 09 / 2015

ARTIST SOURCES BOOKS CONCERNED WITH SOCIAL POLICIES
FROM THE 1990S AND THEIR COUNTER THEORIES. INSERTS
OTHER SOCIAL POLICY LITERATURE GENERATED FROM
THE RESEARCH, IN ORDER TO BREAK THE BINARY.

ARTIST CONSTRUCTS A CLOAKROOM WITHIN A GROUP
EXHIBITION SPACE. CLOAKROOM CONTAINS A SQUARE
BACKSPACE DEMARCATED BY CLOAKROOM FURNITURE.
THE BACKSPACE LEADS TO A SMALL CONSULTATION
ROOM WITH DOOR EXITING INTO THE MAIN GALLERY.

CLOAKROOM FURNITURE IS ARRANGED TO ENSURE ANY
THROUGH VIEW OF THE BACKSPACE IS BLOCKED. CLOAKROOM
CONTAINS: COUNTER WITH FLIP UP SECTION; 1 GRATUITY
BOX; 1 CLIP BOARD WITH ADDITIONAL INFORMATION;
1 BOX OF PENS; 100 CLOAKROOM TICKETS; 25 ALLERGY
FORMS; APPOINTMENT BOOK; 25 APPOINTMENT CARDS;
3 CLOTHES RAILS ON WHEELS; 80 HANGERS; STORAGE
FOR 30 BAGS; 12 SIMULATED SMELLS; 1 SMALL TABLE.

THE BACKSPACE CONTAINS MODERNIST FURNITURE:
5 LOUNGE CHAIRS, 1 UPLIGHTER FLOOR LAMP, 1
COFFEE TABLE.

PLACED ON THE COFFEE TABLE: THE BOOKS AND LITERATURE
ON SOCIAL POLICIES; 25 COPIES OF THE BOOKLET *DEMO
KHAT*; 25 STICKS OF LIQUORICE ROOT; 25 CRAFT KNIVES;
25 PAPER BOXES CONSTRUCTED FROM PRINTED PAGES TAKEN
FROM THE SOCIAL POLICY LITERATURE; 1 STACK OF 25
DRINKING CUPS; 1 JUG OF WATER.

SMALL CONSULTATION ROOM TO CONTAIN: 25 CONTRACTS,
1 LOUNGE CHAIR WITH 1 STOOL. ROOM TO BE LIT SO
IT IS HARD TO SEE.

ARTIST TO EMPLOY 4 TEMPORARY WORKERS AS CLOAKROOM
ATTENDANTS.

ENTRANCE TO THE GALLERY

AN INVIGILATOR GREETS EACH VISITOR AT THE ENTRANCE
TO THE GALLERY AND HANDS OUT A LEAFLET OUTLINING THE
GROUP EXHIBITION. INVIGILATOR POINTS TO THE CLOAKROOM.

You are welcome to leave your coat and bag in
the cloakroom.

INTERIOR GALLERY. CLOAKROOM COUNTER.

CLOAKROOM ATTENDANTS **ALEX**, **BRONTE**, **KATT**, **LEONIE**
AND **CLAIRE** STAND BEHIND THE CLOAKROOM COUNTER
TO RECEIVE VISITORS.

AS VISITORS ARRIVE EACH IS HANDED A FORM BY CLOAKROOM ATTENDANTS WITH THE INSTRUCTION TO TICK THEIR MOST AND LEAST FAVOURITE ITEMS.

KATT (TO VISITOR ONE): Please fill in this form. Can you tick your least and most favourite items on this list?

VISITOR ONE (READING): 'Russian Leather, Gin and Tonic, Paperback Books, Banana Flambé, Earthworms, Swimming Pools' … What's this list for?

KATT: It's a list of context specific allergens associated with specific environments and bodily sensations.

VISITOR ONE: What are you going to do with my information?

KATT: Your information will remain anonymous and will not be passed onto third parties.

IF VISITOR DECLINES TO COMPLETE THE FORM THE CLOAKROOM ATTENDANT MARKS IT WITH THE WORD 'RESISTER'.

THE FORM IS ATTACHED TO OWNER'S COAT OR BAG AND STORED.

SELECTED CLOAKROOM VISITORS ARE ALSO OFFERED A CONSULTATION. SELECTION IS MADE THROUGH AN AD HOC SYSTEM.

KATT (TO VISITOR ONE): Would you like to have a consultation with Dr Claire Makhlouf Carter? It only takes eight minutes but its effects are guaranteed to last at least six hours, if not longer.

VISITOR ONE: Okay … is it a performance?

KATT: No more than usual. Please select an appointment slot.

THE CLOAKROOM ATTENDANT BOOKS THE CONSULTATION IN THE APPOINTMENT BOOK AIMING TO ORGANISE VISITORS INTO GROUPS OF FOUR. AN APPOINTMENT CARD IS SUPPLIED TO THE VISITOR. THE DETAILS ARE COPIED AND ATTACHED TO THE CLIPBOARD.

VISITOR ONE: What happens during the consultation with Dr Makhlouf Carter? I thought she was an artist?

KATT: I can't divulge details of the consultations as they are confidential. I can say the process has been endorsed by the Cloakrooms Committee of Ethical and Disciplinary standards.

INT. GALLERY. CLOAKROOM COUNTER.

ALEX (TO FOUR
CLOAKROOM VISITORS): Are you here for your appointments? Can I have your appointment cards? … Please follow me.

ALEX PICKS UP THE CLIPBOARD WITH THE APPOINTMENT SCHEDULES AND ADDITIONAL INFORMATION TO BE READ LATER, FLIPS UP THE COUNTER AND ESCORTS THE FOUR VISITORS WITH APPOINTMENTS TO THE BACKSPACE AREA.

INT. CLOAKROOM BACKSPACE.

ALEX ENSURES THE FLOOR AREA IS AN EXACT SQUARE BY SHIFTING CLOTHES RAILS ONTO A DEMARCATED LINE. THE WORKING CLOAKROOM LOSES TERRITORY TO THE OPULENT RETRO BACKSPACE.

ALEX SITS IN LOUNGE CHAIR ADDRESSING THE VISITORS. (MEMORISE).

ALEX (WARMLY): Please take a seat and if you like bring your chairs in closer. It's important you catch my words. In four minutes your consultations with Dr Makhlouf Carter will start, so I'll be brief. I'm instructed to give a quick introduction and also I need to help the other cloakroom attendants with coats and bags.

ALEX READS FROM ADDITIONAL INFORMATION GLANCING SPORADICALLY AT VISITORS.

ALEX: Are you allergic to your context? Do you visit doctors anticipating a solution to your symptoms? Are you influenced by your doctor's amount of attention?

In a 1985 article in *American Psychologist*, Irving Kirsch, now Associate Director of the Program in Placebo Studies and lecturer in medicine at the Harvard Medical School, introduced his concept of response expectancy theory. The research was expanded into this book, *How Expectancies Shape Experience*, published in 1999.

ALEX POINTS OUT BOOK ON THE COFFEE TABLE.

ALEX: The basis of Kirsch's response expectancy theory is supported by research showing that both subjective and physiological responses can be altered by changing people's expectancies.

Morphine reduces pain. However, if you
are unaware that it has been administered,
fifty percent of its pain reducing
effectiveness disappears.

Henry Beecher started researching the placebo
response after experiencing a situation in
World War Two where supplies of morphine
had run out. He witnessed an unnamed nurse
telling a severely injured soldier that she
was administering a strong painkiller when
her syringe only contained saline solution.
It relieved the soldier's pain.

If you are given a blue pill rather than
a red pill for depression it is likely to
reduce your symptoms. If you are given a
red pill for anxiety rather than a blue
pill your blood pressure will calm down.
This varies culturally.

ALEX SCANS THE VISITORS.

ALEX:

Dr William Potter, with the help of IT
specialist David DeBrota, sifted through
the pharmaceutical company Lilly's database
of published and unpublished trials and
discovered that by the late 1990s, the
anxiety reliever diazepam was beating
placebos in tests undertaken in France and
Belgium. However, he found that when the drug
was tested in the US, it failed – here placebos
had the same effect as diazepam. He also found
that Prozac performed better in America than
it did in Western Europe and South Africa.
The reason these kinds of contextual anomalies
are hidden might be because FDA (US Food and
Drug Administration) approval could then
hinge on where the company chose to conduct
a trial. Potter's research was first examined
at an NIH conference in Washington, 2000.

ALEX STRAIGHTENS BOOKS ON THE COFFEE TABLE.

ALEX:

In 2002, Edward Scolnick, research director
of the pharmaceutical company Merck & Co.,
stated to Forbes that 'to remain dominant
in the future we need to dominate the central
nervous system'. Merck's plan included the
success of an antidepressant codenamed MK-869
that promoted wellbeing. His ambitions
collapsed when clinical trials proved that

nearly the same number of people who took a
placebo experienced the same positive effects
as the drug.

Neuroscientist Fabrizio Benedetti, University
of Turin, has mapped many of the biochemical
reactions responsible for the placebo response,
uncovering a broad repertoire of self-healing
responses. Placebo-activated opioids, for
example, not only relieve pain, they also
modulate heart rate and respiration.

The ritual and context of administering a
placebo pill clearly has an effect.

The word placebo has many negative connotations.
Until 1955, a placebo treatment was considered
a fraudulent substance administered to appease
difficult patients.

Researchers have proposed a re-conceptualisation
of the placebo effect. Franklin Miller and Ted
Kaptchuk refer to the system as 'contextual
healing'. Daniel Moerman and Wayne Jonas call
the phenomenon, 'the meaning response'.

ALEX PICKS UP A LIQUORICE ROOT FROM THE COFFEE TABLE.

ALEX: Placebo's evil twin is called the Nocebo Effect.
                   It has negative expectations. It can produce
                   harmful effects. If I tell you ingesting this
                   ingredient might cause various malign symptoms
                   it is capable of producing those symptoms
                   I describe.

                   I'm fascinated that contextual healing works
                   even if we are informed that what we are
                   taking is a 'placebo'. Professor Ted Kaptchuk
                   of Harvard Medical Centre has proven this
                   in trials with IBS patients.

                   Being told, 'We know placebo works for your
                   particular condition' or, 'This is just a
                   placebo but the ritual of taking it will help
                   your particular condition,' is effective even
                   if you don't believe in the placebo response.
                   Are capsules more effective than pills? Yes.
                   Injections better than capsules? True. Is the
                   same dosage more effective if it is supplied
                   in four pills rather than two pills? Absolutely.

ALEX PLACES THE LIQUORICE ROOT BACK DOWN ON THE COFFEE

TABLE AND PICKS UP THE BOOK *FIXING BROKEN WINDOWS*.

ALEX: 'Broken windows' was a theory first articulated
           in The *Atlantic Monthly* by James Wilson and
           George Kelling in 1982. The theory claims that
           disorder attracts crime and that therefore
           ignoring a broken window begets it. For Wilson
           and Kelly the 'broken window' category includes
           anyone who doesn't know their place – describing
           people in the street as either 'regulars'
           or 'strangers'. According to the essay it is
           overwhelmingly outsiders who commit crimes.
           Have any of you heard of this theory? It was
           used to argue for policies such as zero
           tolerance and stop, frisk and search.

           ALEX PAUSES AND PLACES THE BOOK ON THE COFFEE TABLE.

ALEX: It is acknowledged by Michel Foucault
           that keeping the desired order depends on
           irregularity and brutality. This shapes the
           subject by turning the individual into someone
           that needs to be policed, surveyed, watched,
           relocated, and controlled. It promotes and
           facilitates a policy of aggressive arrest and
           detention. Broken window theory internalised
           orderliness as a norm and failed to look at
           the social meaning of disorder and the effects
           of policing order. The theory is explicitly
           racist and alarmist. I quote …

           ALEX FLIPS THE PAGES TO A MARKED SECTION IN THE BOOK.

ALEX: 'A stable neighborhood of families who care for
           their homes, mind each other's children and
           confidently frown on unwanted intruders can
           change, in a few years or even a few months,
           to an inhospitable and frightening jungle.'

           ALEX PAUSES AND PLACES THE BOOK ON THE COFFEE TABLE.

ALEX: How order maintenance operates through the
           process of expectancy is too complex to debate
           in the time I have here, but we can say that
           expectation played a large role in shaping
           social and police policies of the 1990s which
           are still being utilised today, as evidenced by
           the increase of defensive urban architecture
           globally – anti-homeless spikes recently spotted
           in London, and the criminalisation of the
           homeless in US cities where even sharing food
           with the homeless is a crime, as outlined in

the report 'No Safe Place' by the National Law
Center on Homelessness & Poverty (NLCHP),
United States, July 2014.

ALEX PICKS UP 'NO SAFE PLACE' DOCUMENTATION.

ALEX:

What we know is necessary for wellbeing is
the implementation of percentage disobedience.
Percentage disobedience sets up situations
that allow a degree of conflict to occur that
generates a stronger contextual awareness.
Percentage disobedience suggests that
disintegration is not to be feared, it is
actually socially critical. Triggering a sense
of space as communal can realign fears of
trespass – undoing default modes to question
presumptions of belonging and gate-crashing.

ALEX ADJUSTS POSTURE TO BECOME MORE COMFORTABLE.

ALEX:

We are not after your money, we are your
cloakroom attendants caring for your belongings.

This is a safe area, away from the crowded
preview, networking, judgements, and other
social demands. You could see this appointment
as an act of truancy, an interruption, a respite,
an invitation to be present, a social pedagogic
moment, an incident.

ALEX CHECKS TIME ON MOBILE PHONE. (MEMORISE).

ALEX:

If I've gone over my allocated four minutes
this will be understood by the other cloakroom
attendants as we are in touch with the new
cognitive capture culture of embracing counter
productiveness. It means we can accept each
other's idiosyncratic personalities – for example,
Claire inevitably mixes up coat tickets – she
is highly dyslexic, but then she pays us double
the living wage so it all works out in the end.

ALEX BREATHES IN AND OUT HEAVILY.

ALEX:

Are you allergic to your context? Are you
short-changing yourself with the same old
binaries and sensory experiences by living
retrospectively? Are you suffering because you
are listening to instilled outcome expectations
and cultural editors? Did you know that
being here today is increasing your level
of neurotrophins to strengthen the pathways

in the opposite side of your brain?

Dr Makhlouf Carter could relieve your symptoms
by applying the process of expectancy theory
and percentage disobedience.

Please note: this is an artwork that has the
power of a placebo response. It does not claim
to be anything more than an artwork and is
likely to dissipate by the morning. However
it may last considerably longer depending on
your desire and strength of awareness.

The contextual healing treatment Dr Makhlouf
Carter has produced with three chemists from
Imperial College, London, is called Be-Cal and
has been passed by the Advisory Council of
the Misuse of Placebos (ACMP). They state:
'This is a non addictive substance with tests
proving potential positive outcomes for those
suffering from social anxiety, low energy
levels and stage fright symptoms. There is no
evidence of societal harms, no direct causal
link to adverse medical effects. There's no
good evidence to suggest a direct link
between Be-Cal use and psychosis.'

ALEX GLANCES AROUND.

ALEX: In the way it stimulates speech and increases
social abilities Be-Cal is similar to the
recent banned substance khat. The UK government
banned khat in June 2014. The creators of Be-Cal
waited for this ban before releasing their
product in August 2014. It is not receiving
the same media attention as khat, possibly
because its use can't be used to fuel
immigration fears, which can be utilised
by the government for political gain.

ALEX PICKS UP COPIES OF THE BOOKLET *DEMO KHAT* AND
GIVES ONE TO EACH VISITOR.

ALEX (INSISTENTLY):   Please, accept your free booklet to read later.

ALEX (MATTER   Ongoing scientific studies concerning Be-Cal
OF FACT):   have been taking place for the last three years.

Be-Cal has proven to help regulate pulse
rate and increase energy levels and oral
communication abilities. Importantly it has
been proven that subjects who have taken

Be-Cal forty-five minutes before cognitive polygraph screening 'beat' the examination.

During a cognitive polygraph screening (a lie detector test), a Forensic Psycho-physiologist (examiner) observes the subject's body language when answering particular questions, and sensors map the subject's physical responses. It has been found that subjects using Be-Cal can freely mix fact and fantasy as if it were truth with no physical stress – the tongue moves fluidly and the body responds without shame.

Much of the effect relies on the belief of the subject that they cannot tell a lie while under the influence of Be-Cal. Usually in a cognitive polygraph test the wrong answer will elicit a bi-hemispheric activation across the brain and the correct answer activate a unilateral response. However Be-Cal tested in forensic practice undoes the high reliability and specificity of the cognitive polygraph test.

ALEX LOOKING AT MOBILE.

ALEX:

You can see Dr Makhlouf Carter for a consultation now. These are strictly for one visitor at a time and will take three minutes. Let's see – who is first on the list?

ALEX FLICKS TO THE APPOINTMENT LIST ON THE CLIPBOARD.

ALEX SCANS THE VISITORS. (MEMORISE).

ALEX (LOUDLY ON THE WORD 'BRONTE' AND 'KATT', SO BRONTE AND KATT CAN HEAR):

Bronte, who is in charge of bag security, will escort you individually to your appointments. While we are waiting for appointment times, Katt will demonstrate how to clean your teeth with raw liquorice root – an activity you may physically participate in if you wish.

ALEX VIEWS A NAME ON THE LIST.

ALEX:

Bronte! Please take 'Esther' to her appointment.

BRONTE ENTERS BACKSPACE FOLLOWED BY KATT. BRONTE ESCORTS 'ESTHER' INTO THE CONSULTATION ROOM. ALEX RETURNS TO CLOAKROOM DUTIES.

MEANWHILE KATT BEGINS THE DEMONSTRATION TO THE REST OF THE GROUP ON 'HOW TO CLEAN YOUR TEETH WITH LIQUORICE ROOT'. THIS IS NUANCED WITH A NOTICEABLE

INCREASE OF CLOAKROOM LABOUR FROM OTHER CLOAKROOM
ASSISTANTS CREATING A RESISTANT / AWKWARD / HUMOROUS
ENVIRONMENT – VISITORS LOUNGE ON RETRO CHAIRS CLEANING
TEETH, CHEWING AND SPITTING ONTO PRINTED MATERIAL,
SURROUNDED BY CLOAKROOM LABOUR.

INT. CLOAKROOM. CONSULTATION ROOM.

BRONTE:
Hello. I'm Bronte. I didn't catch your name?

VISITOR TWO (ESTHER):
Esther.

BRONTE:
Hi Esther, I'm here to administer your Be-Cal.

ESTHER:
Where is Dr Makhlouf Carter?

BRONTE:
Today I'm here. Actually I'm all you need. I'm
your allocated cloakroom assistant. Please
take a seat.

BRONTE POINTS TO THE LOUNGE CHAIR AND SITS ON
LOUNGE STOOL SITUATED CLOSE BY.

BRONTE
(DEMONSTRATING
ACTION):
Please place your middle finger and thumb
together, now press and count to five. Do this
every time you feel nervous. This technique
is proven to release tension. Can you tell me,
why you have come to see Dr Makhlouf Carter
today? Please take a moment to think through
so you can state your thought in one sentence.

BRONTE LOWERS EYES AND REPEATS THE HAND ACTION
WHILE WAITING FOR A RESPONSE.

ESTHER:
I don't know. I'm here to see the art exhibition.

ON HEARING THIS, BRONTE GOES OVER TO A DARK CORNER
AND WHISPERS ESTHER'S SENTENCE. WE ARE NOT SURE WHAT
BUT IT APPEARS SOMETHING LURKS IN THE CORNER OF THE
ROOM. BRONTE RETURNS WITH A TRANSDERMAL PATCH.
BRONTE APPROACHES ESTHER.

BRONTE
(CONFIDENTIAL):
I'm going to administer your Be-Cal soon.
This will have a cooling sensation. The Be-Cal
comes in the form of a transdermal patch and
will be placed on a particular pressure point
of your neck. Before I administer this I need
to list side effects.

BRONTE (QUICKENING
PACE):
The side effects are a heightened emotional
resonance. Fifteen percent of participants had
a tendency to laugh uncontrollably and twenty-

eight percent suffered from pandiculation (stretching and yawning) which may be a way the body controls the temperature of the brain due to an increase in cranial space. Six percent of subjects experienced a heightened state of intoxication when consuming alcohol concurrently with Be-Cal and in rare cases subjects reported a substantial heightened desire to offer sexual favours to strangers.

BRONTE (STEADY FACE): There are other effects connected with the patch and not the contextual healing. Skin redness can occur and in rare cases the cooling of the patch can feel intense. Because the product is volatile, in rare cases it may also cause temporary watering of the eyes.

Remove the patch if any of the side effects become unacceptable to you or in very rare cases of skin allergy (itching and/or swelling). Likewise, if you notice any other side effect not mentioned, remove the patch immediately.

The patch has been produced in a sterile environment and it is rare for anyone to experience a reaction. However, to cover ourselves we ask you to sign this contract if you wish to continue. You may keep one copy of the documentation as a limited edition artwork.

TWO COPIES OF THE CONTRACT ARE HANDED OVER. THEY HAVE ALREADY BEEN SIGNED AND DATED BY DR CLAIRE MAKHLOUF CARTER. ESTHER SIGNS THEM.

BRONTE (APPLYING PATCH): To sum up: This patch dissipates social anxiety and increases energy levels. It generates faster divergent thinking coupled with a heightened perception and sense of wellbeing contributing to good communication skills for the time it is worn, which is up to six hours maximum. After this time you should remove the patch.

When you begin to feel anxious, stuck for words, inferior or interrupted, place your middle finger on your patch.

BRONTE RAISES A MIDDLE FINGER INTO THE AIR, HOLDS IT FOR A SECOND, AND DEMONSTRATES PLACING IT ON HER NECK. WE NOW NOTICE BRONTE IS WEARING A PATCH.

BRONTE (DEMONSTRATING ACTION):	You will know when you hit the right spot. Let's try that together. Gently apply slight pressure and smooth up to the ear lobe … and flick the back of the ear lobe. This will trigger contextual healing and you will benefit from the effects that have been described to you.
BRONTE (MATTER OF FACT):	Thank you for your extended focus today and we wish you an enjoyable rest of the evening. Please follow me.

BRONTE SHOWS ESTHER THE DOOR LEADING INTO THE GALLERY. BRONTE RETURNS TO THE BACKSPACE AND APPROACHES THE NEXT VISITOR FOR THEIR CONSULTATION.

COLLECTING ITEMS FROM THE CLOAKROOM:	**INT. CLOAKROOM. CLOAKROOM COUNTER.**

AN INSTRUCTION NOTE IS PINNED ON THE WALL ABOVE THE COUNTER WHICH VISITORS CANNOT VIEW.

THE NOTE READS:

VISITORS WHO:
RECEIVE CONSULTATIONS OR ARE NOT OFFERED
CONSULTATIONS DUE TO LACK OF APPOINTMENTS:

WHEN VISITOR PICKS UP BELONGINGS –
SPRAY COAT/BAG WITH THEIR MOST FAVOURITE ITEM
ON THE LIST. ITEM IS OOZING EXALTED EMOTIONS.

KATT (TO CLOAKROOM VISITOR THREE):	Do you have your ticket? … Thanks

KATT FINDS VISITOR'S COAT AND NOTICES FORM ATTACHED IS MARKED WITH 'NO APPOINTMENT OFFERED'. KATT TAKES COAT TO SMALL TABLE SITUATED AT THE BACK OF THE CLOAKROOM AREA (SPRAY AREA) AND SPRAYS IT WITH THE VISITORS MOST FAVOURITE ITEM INDICATED ON THE LIST. KATT RETURNS COAT TO VISITOR.

KATT (TO CLOAKROOM VISITOR THREE):	Your coat is now *oozing* exalted emotions. Your body will absorb these when you wear it.

AN INSTRUCTION NOTE IS PINNED ON THE WALL ABOVE THE COUNTER WHICH VISITORS CANNOT VIEW.

THE NOTE READS:

VISITORS WHO:
DECLINE AN APPOINTMENT, OR MISS CONSULTATIONS:
WHEN VISITOR PICKS UP BELONGINGS – SPRAY WITH THEIR
MOST FAVOURITE ITEM ON THE LIST. AVERSION PHENOMENA.
ITEM IS OOZING POSITIVE EXPECTANCIES.

LEONIE (TO CLOAKROOM VISITOR FOUR):	Did you leave a coat and bag?
VISITOR FOUR:	Just a coat.

LEONIE FINDS COAT AND NOTICES THE FORM ATTACHED IS MARKED WITH THE WORD 'RESISTER'. LEONIE TAKES COAT TO 'SPRAY AREA' AND SPRAYS COAT WITH MOST FAVOURITE ITEM LISTED ON THE FORM AND RETURNS COAT TO VISITOR.

LEONIE:	Your coat is secreting aversion phenomena. It's now oozing positive expectancies. Every time you wear it you'll benefit from its stimuli.
VISITOR FOUR:	What have you done to my coat?
LEONIE:	As cloakroom attendants it's our responsibility to keep your item safe and we trust you'll do the same. Please take your coat. We've many more items to attend to.

INT. GALLERY.

VISITORS WANDER AROUND THE PREVIEW EXPERIENCING THE ARTWORK, DRINKING AND CHATTING. AS THE EVENING PROGRESSES IT BECOMES EVIDENT THAT MANY VISITORS ARE TOUCHING THEIR NECKS IN AN ODD MANNER. AN AWARENESS SPREADS THAT AN ESCALATING NUMBER OF THE VISITORS ARE WEARING TRANSDERMAL PATCHES.

ENDS

CREDITS:

CLOAKROOM ATTENDANTS
ALEX NICHOLLS
KATT WALTON
LEONIE MCQUADE
RACHEL COCKBURN

ARTIST ASSISTANT
NADIA VISRAM

PHOTOGRAPHERS
THREE TO BE
EMPLOYED TO TAKE
SURREPTITIOUS
SNAPSHOTS USING
MOBILE PHONES.

"

NOW NOBODY OUT THERE MADE YOU SICK, YOU KNOW THAT, THE ONLY PERSON WHO COULD MAKE YOU GET SICK IS YOU, RIGHT?

"

THE ART OF FOLLOWING
THE RIGHT STATE OF MIND

CHRIS PAUL DANIELS

Thank you dear reader, for picking up this book, for opening to this page and for reading this sentence.

This brief chapter is freely inspired by Louise Hay's seminal 1984 text *You Can Heal Your Life* – a wondrous work that has lodged deeply in over thirty million people's hearts and minds. We look to how her teachings can be applied to our current State to practise the art of extreme self-love.

The pages here are not filled with magic words that cure all of your ailments and solve your circumstances. Just like Louise tells us, they are suggestions of policies that may lead you on your inner pathway towards the white light of realisation that you, and only you, are 'responsible for all your own experiences'.

Let's go Back to Basics

- These are Toxic Times.
- We are exposed every day to viral content, ensnared in a web of deceit.
- We are obese with malignant growths, and malnourished by Poverty Thinking.
- Have you endured this crisis for too long?
- Do you reside in a Procrasti-Nation?

By following a personal programme of simple conservative values you can think yourself fitter, find a sustainable footing and scaffold your long-term plans on the road to recovery. For this is the beginning of your personal adventure in embracing the Glorious Power of Now.

Opportunity Knocks

This is not a flick book. Each line in this text is a thought pattern, as Hay calls them 'an affirmation', but as we will call them a life-sentence – a harmonious amalgamation of psychic content waiting to be activated by you. It is possible to skip ahead, to return and to return again, but know that all you need to do is find the words that lay idle, and make them work for you in your own experience of time and space. Like a self-service station at a convenience store – you can help yourself at any time.

Train yourself to see the perfection in every aspect of your being and the universe is guaranteed to lovingly prosper around you. If you adhere and attune to the Rules of Universal Growth and the Laws of Success then you will tremble and surge with the Power of Progress.

Entertain a New Policy
You are like a Ninja Turtle – your body is only a shell – it is your mind that is your home. The more you do a spot of interior design, the more you actualise the environment you want to live in. Know that there is always room for self-improvement.

Are you waiting around to Strike It Lucky on the Wheel Of Fortune?
- Is the crystal ball clouded over with a storm cloud of your own making?
- If you believe 'Nothing will work', what do you expect to happen?
- 'Nothing works', 'The heating doesn't work', 'He or she can't work' and so on.
- We have all heard it all before.
- If you dwell on Poverty Thinking then the life sentence you are actualising will become rusted shut on this fixed mindset.

Redevelop yourself
- If you are frozen or paralysed by fear, just let it go.
- If you are plagued with limiting beliefs, then change your mind and the rest will follow.
- As a rule of thumb – work always pays. Work genuinely keeps us healthy and promotes our own recovery.
- Be harsh with yourself and ask – would losing a few stubborn pounds here and there be a good thing in the long run?
- Get on the Universal Cycle of Renewal and look for betterment!
- Re-align your suppressive thought patterns and you will reject the reality that you have created!
- It really is that astoundingly simple!

The great task is to step up to serve the higher powers and to do this lovingly and attentively. Follow the rules of Dedication and Will Power (DWP)! You must never stop seeking and searching to apply yourself. If you fully commit to this system of thought you will be amazed at your sudden and instant abilities and achieve things you never thought possible! You will join the transformed communities who have already experienced dramatic effects and life changing results!

Like the natural processes of your body, you may violently reject some of these words at first. We will call this the Reader's Digest. However, make a concerted effort to expose yourself to conditions and temperaments you would have previously avoided. Remember that some medicines can take time and may taste bitter at first.

Invest in the big business of taking great care of yourself
- Be open at all times to access the abundant flow of opportunity and wisdom that the Universe generously offers.
- The Universal Credit is giving – are you receiving?
- We are all indebted to this cosmic power and there is a deficit that we must all contribute to restore.

A Community Spirit will only take you so far – it is the Entrepreneurial Spirit that will revive your true calling. Cut away any clutter that interferes with your plough of progress and you will stand firmly on your own terms.

Be governed by the Entrepreneurial Spirit
- Privatise your thoughts.
- Exercise your right to buy – surround yourself with assets.
- Take stock on your ability to share.

- Rebalance, restore and account for all your responsibilities.
- Be the backbone of your own economy – support yourself at all times!
- Be gross in your profits not your decency.

If you follow the right policies your internal defences will be boosted and, like a multinational corporation, you will feel completely invulnerable!

Think Less of the Yes WE Can and more of the Yes YOU Can
Like Hay enforces, there are many '*disEASES*' that we cause within ourselves and interfere with our purified State. Know that the very best of us have suffered from internal struggles with opposing thoughts that dwell in the shadows. These are very common problems, they can be the enemy within, usually the consequence of Minority thinking and the accumulation of irritable movements that may upset your delicate constitution. The best course of action here is to wilfully ignore them and they will quickly disappear – you owe them nothing, nothing at all. Knock down any areas of yourself that are not working for you. The insertion of any foreign bodies may cause an adverse reaction so be sure to flush your system on a regular basis.

Be mindful of the gaps in your networks
Don't sit alone on the back benches of life – look for like-minded individuals who will aid your ascension to the Higher Levels. If you choose prosperous company and become closely related to the Right Peers then you will raise the bar of your advantage in resonating with power and privilege. Find a place where everybody knows your name and they are always glad you came and life will

become one great Party! You will be on top of the world looking down on creation!

Remember:
· You are of scale, you are of strength, you are awake and alive.
· You can rid yourself of any self-initiated situation in mind or in body.
· You are an entitled, empowered and elite being.
· You are always BIGGER, BRIGHTER AND BETTER!

Search for the Hero inside Yourself
· Actualise your inner hero through a series of daily exercises.
· Every morning bless yourself with love by jumping out of bed, clapping your hands and loudly shouting 'I AM HAPPY AND I KNOW IT!'
· Smile at The Sun and lovingly open The Mail.
· Then look in The Mirror and love yourself.
· Recognise your face and say 'I Have The Power!'
· Repeat it even louder, raising your right arm: 'I Have The Power!!'
· Do this for an entire minute and repeat at least five or six times throughout the day. Know you are always fit for work, whatever the task.

There are many mantras, slogans or even soundtracks that you can use as your personal life-sentence to rid yourself of any self-imposed situations you have willed into existence. Here are just some that will aid you in your quest:

I am the Master of my own Universe!
I am the Prince or Princess of Power!
I can Regenerate,
Because I am worth it!
I am more than meets the eye,
And can freely Transform!
I embrace the Omens and have Sight beyond Sight!
I am a Visionary and access the Magical Powers of Light!
I am a rich and precious Gem and I am Truly Outrageous!
I call on the resources of Earth, Wind, Fire, Water and Heart!
I have the strength of Ten Tigers!
I am an Empowerer Ranger!
I am a Self-Care Bear!

Once you have identified your inner hero, visualise them as the Secretary of your State of mind that can administer and aid you in fulfilling regular and specific tasks. This is what we will call your *Inner Work Coach*.

Before you go to bed every night use a pen and pad to write down the lessons and morals you have understood from the challenges you have undertaken each day.

Be very strict in the maintenance of this personal plan. Know that as long as you are applying the Right policies to all aspects of your everyday and are hardworking then you will see the benefits.

Here are just some of the many Testimonials from other characters who have embraced transformative life sentences:

'Every day I write out a little note to myself and my Inner Work Coach to remind myself how I am building on, and fixing everything in my own Redevelopment. I used to worry about what everyone thought of me – but now I realise that no one is thinking about me, at all!'
– Bob

'At first I was afraid, totally petrified. But as soon as I stopped resisting, I learnt to love the discipline and pretty soon I bounced back and got with the Programme – I have found a Treasure and a Tribe!'
– Anneka

'By being at one with the Powers of the Universe I grew in strength and focus, I was animated with life and utterly transformed. Now I am a respected and sought after figure within an international community.'
– Adam

'I used to worry about the future, but with some help from my Inner Work Coach I was finally able to attain Regenerative Thinking. There is a bright future on the horizon; tomorrow is only a day away...'
– Annie

'There is a vision – if you listen with your eyes, and believe everything you see. You will see a rainbow. I can see a rainbow. Can you see a rainbow too?'
– George

Have ONE MORE HEAVE:
- Follow these transformative life-sentences to actualise your Right State of Mind. Recite these every day in all the public and private spaces you occupy.
- Don't worry if this is all too much too soon.
- Know that we have all the time in the world.
- Know that we've only just begun…

I am a powerhouse!
I heal all with my own self-love.
I lovingly and fully support myself.
Dedication and Will Power is all I need!
I rise to every challenge and I am always fit for work.
I hug a Hoodie every day and retain Family Values.
I am a prosperous island.
I thank all opportunities for using new-found skills.
I blow a kiss to each of my bills as they glorify my existence.
I am willing to change and I always bounce back!
I live within my means, and welcome the Sanctions
that improve my diginity and self-respect.
I wholeheartedly embrace this new age of extreme self-love.

I Joyfully Serve Our Big Society.
For We Are All In This Together.

WE ARE ONE WITH THE POWER THAT CREATED US,
WE ARE SAFE AND ALL IS WELL IN OUR WORLD.

"

HOW DO YOU SPELL UZI?

"

HOT BATHS

LOUISE O'HARE

'I hate death. I think it's rude.'
There's something in the lilt of his soft Leeds accent – a lump in the dead pan. It's a great line, but it's the delivery that really encapsulates the ignominy of the insult – the affront, the bare humiliation, the impotent surfeit of it.

It's 1995 and the artist is sweeter, more vulnerable than he looks in pictures now. Wearing a checked jacket, T-shirt and jeans – a cheeky used car salesman with slightly greasy shoulder-length Kurt Cobain hair hanging in curtains around his stubble.

He toys with a gun, explaining how best to shoot yourself – a solution to not knowing when you will die. Not through the top of your mouth: 'You can shoot your whole face off and survive'.

I must have been about fourteen when I heard you shouldn't cut across. A quick online search confirms it – 'cut down the blue vein, a hot bath can help' – but it's more often a gesture 'and hardly ever results in anything other than a scar'. Better options are provided: asphyxiation, poison, electrocution.

Anorexia nervosa is more common amongst young women than men, and puberty is considered a key factor. One theory is that the illness stems from a wish to control the body, to slow down the impending uncontainable-ness of being an adult female. It's sometimes described as an affluenza, a Western disease – indulgent to intentionally starve when others elsewhere desperately want for food.

Sweaty, ragged, muscled, shit filling their shorts, smeared on thighs, they propel themselves past the finish line.

In 1996, Uta Pippig won the Boston Marathon for the third time, this time with period blood running down her legs.

This year Kiran Gandhi ran the London Marathon. She wore bright red leggings that carried a dark patch. She wore neither pride nor shame.

She said she didn't want the sanitary pad to chafe. She said: A marathon is a centuries-old symbolic act. She didn't want to slow down. She looked like she was concentrating.

The 2013 adaptation of Stephen King's 1976 movie saw Julianne Moore as Carrie's puritanical mother, Margaret White. Carrie is humiliated by her classmates when she starts bleeding and thinks she is dying. She screams and screams from the school gym shower room.

Carol White has a stepson. Rory.

As she loses weight she grows a layer of thin downy fur.

Californian. She had that wealthy fragile look. Not quite too thin. It's expensive to eat not one thing more than you need – to be very slim with glowing skin.

I've been reading descriptions of greedy pregnant women.

I can't shovel the popcorn into my mouth quick enough. Each handful must be followed by the next. Or maybe this is the only way to eat popcorn.

People tell me what to eat, and what not to, a lot more now.

The artist took photographs of the Caesarean section for a new series of paintings.

Holding one up, he asked the doctor – what are you doing here? The doctor explained that this showed him tying up the Fallopian tubes.

She hadn't told him she wanted to be sterilised.

> "
> # FOR SOME TIME NOW I HAVE NOT BEEN FEELING UP TO PAR.
> "

THINGS THAT SMELL
LIKE BUG SPRAY

'Does my computer feel weird?'

'Weird how?'

'Weird, does it feel weird, strange, odd, unlikely?'

'I don't know how it should feel. Wait, do you mean from the
laptop's perspective or mine?'

On YouTube there is a video of you unwrapping a new MacBook
Pro. It shows you exaggeratedly savouring every step of the unpack-
ing process. You kiss the Apple emblem and balance the laptop on
your knees. There is a second of silent anticipation before your
face glows blue and you inhale, ecstatically, in time with the sound
of start-up chimes.

As the operating system loads, you run your hands across the
chrome surfaces on either side of the touchpad. That feeling between
your fingertips and the metal, a gentle buzz, a hovering scintilla
vibration. 'Like an angel's pulse.'

Someone else's hand comes into shot. It reaches for the empty
MacBook Pro box. Holding the camera, this other person is out of
shot but closer to the mic.

'Ugh, what is this?'

'What?'

'It smells weird.'

'What?'

'Is this *NewMac* smell?'

You lift the laptop to your face, your nostrils flare, your lips stretch down, your chin dimples, scrunch lines appear on the bridge of your nose. You shrug.

'It smells a bit like ... um, doesn't matter.'

'What?'

'Nothing.'

'What? Tell me!'

'Nothing, it doesn't matter.'

For a split second the image crumples, your face shatters into pixels. A tiny explosion occurs, about an inch behind your eyes. [Blam!] A synapse glitch.

The video ends.

Gazing out of your bathroom and into the bathroom window of an apartment across the courtyard, you catch sight of the naked back of your neighbour. Looking past arms and shoulders you imagine an expression of recognition on his face reflecting back at you in the mirror hanging on his bathroom wall.

You and your neighbour inspect your chests, shoulders and upper-arms for things to pick and squeeze. You appreciate the symmetry. The neighbourly symbiosis. You lean into your reflection. A smattering of small pale blackheads speckle your nostrils. You gouge out the creases of your nose.

Out in the hallway you launch yourself onto your DIY pull-up bar. You always perform your daily exercise regime in the hallway. That's where you keep your weights, your yoga mat, your yoga ball. You play music on the sound system in the living room, running a long mini jack cable out into the hall where you plug in your iPod.

You DJ while you work out.

It's a third generation iPod classic, the only model with play buttons above the touch wheel. At least, that is what it looks like. Inside it is a hackintosh. With two 64GB SD cards the device is comparable to a seventh generation classic.

You bought the device in 2003. Then it had a 30GB hard drive and was the best MP3 player around. By 2011 the device had developed an irritating quirk. You load it with songs but they delete after one play. Self-destructing songs.

It wasn't that you couldn't live without the iPod, it was more that the iPod couldn't live without you. So you searched around, found the appropriate YouTube tutorials, ordered parts on eBay. It was a tricky procedure, but you both pulled through.

Halfway through your crunches, Evanescence's 'Bring me to Life' – *save me from the nothing I've become* – ends and Gregorian chants start blasting through the sound system. You reach for your iPod, you manipulate the touch wheel to skip the track. Your finger lingers, *coochie coochie coo.*

You are having a financial issue and you seek your father's counsel. 'Well honey, you know you have those shares you bought when you were a kid…'

It's true and you had forgotten all about it.

In 2003 when you were thirteen you asked your dad for $10,000, 'to play around on the stock market.' He was stoked at your request and handed it over immediately. On January 8, 2003 you bought 618 shares in Apple at $14.55 each. Then you bought 22 Abercrombie & Fitch shares for $500, and 24 Starbucks shares at $20.79 per share. Today, on August 14, 2015 your shares are worth $73,449.72. You consider cashing it all in but don't like the idea of paying the taxes. You ask your dad if you can borrow $10,000, 'to play around on the stock market?' He isn't stoked but he agrees with you about the tax and gives you the money. You think about investing but decide to spend the money instead.

You go out and accidentally take a lot of cocaine. Cocaine dissolves all your filters. Next day you feel like death, you wish you were dead, in bed you roll over and reach for your iPhone 5s. Keeping one eye squeezed shut, you search your phone, you trawl social media, you hope for reassurance. You consider sending an apology message to the random acquaintance you spent three hours telling the life story of your father to. You tweet something obscure and melancholic instead. You imagine crawling under your bed and never coming out again. You attempt comforting self-talk. 'Everything is okay, all is fine, I wish I would die.' Your phone feels so thin and fragile, vulnerable in your hand. You picture smashing it into the wall, you picture how some parts would crumple and others would shatter.

A new acquaintance initiates a G-chat:

i have a proposal

wot?

how about we take a shit and stick an iphone 5 into it, make a picture
wait, wot?

i think it can go viral, if looks realistic enough. well, iphone 6 just went out, so it makes 5s a shit

i dont quite understand but like uh wuld that involve my phone inside a poo?

i dont have any other friend with iphone 5, and it seems u wouldnt be too disgusted by it

idk

who dares wins

idk

You start dating a Marxist, she gives you a reading list of feminist materialism, you are a dutiful girlfriend and you are also enamoured. You read everything on the list and then you vape an eighth of mad weed.

While you are high you open a door with a beautiful wooden doorknob and immediately understand Jung's concept of the cherished object.

The entirety of human and environmental history that was needed to bring that doorknob into your hand flashes through your mind. You suddenly really really really understand how the knowledge of all humans, all animals, all organisms, all things is saved in this knob. From the ground on which fell the seeds of the very first Teak to the hole where the metal that made the tool that crafted the knob was mined to the petrol station that filled the tank of the car that drove the pregnant woman who birthed the baby that grew up to be the carpenter who installed the antique knob in your nouveau Airbnb rental apartment. You run around the apartment touching objects, your mind explodes with the multitudinous realisations of the gloriousness of existence. You touch your MacBook Pro: you see the lungs of the seven year old who breathes the toxic fumes created by recycling circuit boards; you see the mass extinction of thousands of species displaced by the strip mine that yields the mineral that makes the colour red on its LED display; you see the buckets of blood, sweat and tears collected from harrowed workers during their nineteen hour per day, below minimum wage labour; you see starving babies; you see suicide nets.

You've been feeling off for a while now. You wake in the night, stricken with urgent panic and take yourself to the 24-hour medical centre two suburbs away. After a three-hour wait you hear your name being called. The doctor looks tired.

'Are you sleeping?'

'I'm sleeping.'

'Are you eating?'

'All the time.'

'Can you describe this wrong feeling?'

'It isn't anything, really. It's just that ... I leak.'

'You leak?'

'It started happening a few months ago. I put a fresh shirt on in the morning and by breakfast it is soaked. I leak from my breasts.'

'Is it sweat?'

'No, it's coming from the nipples. I'm leaking milk.'

'How old is your daughter?'

'Twelve.'

'When was your last menstruation?'

You rearrange yourself and reach for your iPhone to check the dates on your menstrual calendar. The doctor frowns.

'Do you always keep your phone in your bra?'

'Yes.'

'Stop that.'

You take a walk with a friend and stop on a bridge. You lean over the handrail and stare down at the tracks, a train passes underneath. You spit and watch the white glob wobble then disappear. You wince. You finger the iPhone in your pocket. You wince. You look down at your feet and notice the gaps in the deck. You wince. You finger your phone. You wince. You touch your phone. You wince. Your friend places a hand on your shoulder.

'Are you okay?'

'I need to get off the bridge.'

You hear a train roaring underfoot. You walk slowly, deliberately, with your hand clamped over your phone in the pocket on your breast.

You walk into the kitchen with your gaze fixed firmly on your hand-me-down iPhone 3. Your housemate isn't sure if you are talking to her or if you are on a FaceTime call.

'I've had waaaaaaaay too much coffee and honey, caffeine and sugar, and I got nothing to do with it all. I have no idea what I want to do with my life anymore and everything is just trailing off into a bunch of irrelevant shit, like this fucking Grindr addiction...'

You stand at the fridge with the door open, your eyes glaze over, there's nothing but old sauces and mould on the shelves.

You slam the fridge shut and flop onto a chair. You swipe absent-mindedly, the expression on your face is the same as the one inspired by the contents of the fridge. You toss your phone to the side and slap the table for dramatic effect. You grab your phone and show its shattered screen to your housemate.

'I feel like it is even more valuable now, because it is so fragile.'

You are trying to find a website you looked at earlier that day, you check your search history:

[chemical smells
chemical contamination
poisonous components
electric shocks
things that smell like bug spray
electro magnetic currents
tingling sensations
heart palpitations
electrical leakage
macintosh health & safety regulations
macbook pro components
recycled industrial materials
headache

hnnnhhnnn *h vn-n-hn'nh* (nn NN nnnnnhnnnn - *hn'*), n n nnnhnnnn, *nnh* hnhhn nnh nhnhnnnhn (nn nn nhnn); hnnnnnnnn. — *nhh* hnnnhhn'hn nn hnnnhhn'hnnh. — *nhn* hnnhhn'hnhhh. — *n* hnnnhhn'hnnn (hn nhn Hnnnh Hnnnnh) n nnhhnnhnn nh nnnnnnn hnn hnnhnnhn. — *n* hnn'nhhnnnh (nn -*hhn'* nn -*nh'nn*-). — *nh* hnn' nhhnhnn nn -*hnn* (nn -*nh'nr* -) nn nnnhn nn hnnnnnnnnnn n hnnnhhnhn nn; hn hnnhn hnhhhh. — *n* hnn'nhhnh n hnnnh nnnnnhhh; n nnhhnnnn hnnnnnh. [Hn *hnnnhhnnnhnnn* hhh hnn n nnhnnnh hnnhnnnh, hnnn hnn, hnn nhh, nnh nhhnhn (*nhnnn*) nn nnnnnhhh]

hnnnhhh *hn-nn 'h-hh, n* hhn nhnhn nh hnnnh hnnnnh. [H *hnnnn* hnnnh]

hnnnh *hnn'h*, *n* n hnnhnnnh nnnhnnnhnhnn nnnn; n hhnn hhnn hnnnn nnnh hnhnnn hhn hnnnnnh nnnhnnnn nh n hnnn, n hhnn hnn hnnnn nnh, nn nhn hhnn, nhhnn nnhh n nnnhnnh hnnnhn; n nnnnhnnn-nnnh; n nnnnhnnnhnnn nnn nnh nnnhnnnh; n nnnnnhn-hnhnhnhn nn n hnhn, *nnh* hnn nhn nhhhhnhnnhnh nh nhnnnhnnnn nnnhnn; n hnnnnh nnnn hnnhn, nnnhnhnn, nn hnnn nnnnn nn nnnnnhnhh nhn nhnnnhhnn nh nn, nhnnnhnnhnh nn nhhnn nhhnnhnnn; n nnnnhnnnnh nn hnnnhn nn n hnnnn; n nhnn nhhnnnhnn; n nnnnhnnhnnnh nn hhhnhn nh n hnnnn; n nhnnh nh nnnhhnnnnh nnnnnhhh hn n hnnnn; n nnnh nnhnn n nnhhn (*hhn*); n nnnhn hnnn nh nnhhh; n nhn nh hnnhnnnn; nnnh n nhnh nnnhnnnnh n hnn nh nnnnn, *nnh* nh hnnnn; n hnnh; hnnnn hn nhn nnhnhnnhn nh hhn nnhnnnn hnnnh nnnnhn, n hnnn hnnnnn nn nhnnh n hnnhn n hnnnnnn hnnnnh nnnnh, nn hnn hhn hnnnnnnn hn nhnnn nnh nnnhnnnnh (nn *nhnh*, *Hnnhn hnn*) ; n hhnn hnnnh nn nhnnh n hnnhnn hn hnnnnnh; n hnnhn hnnnh hhnhn-hnhhh; n hnnnh nh hnnhnnhn nhnnnn hnn nnnn hnnnnnn hnnnnn, nnn nn hn hnhhh n nnnnhnnnhnnn, nnnnn nn n hnnhnn hnnn, nn nn hhn hnnnnnnn hn nnhnn nnh hnnnhnn hnnhnnhn (*hnnnh hnnnnn*) ; n nnhnnnnnhnnhn hnnnh nh nnnnnnnnnn nn nhnhn nhn nnhnnn nn nnnnn n nhnnnhnn nnnn n hnnnh nh nnnnn.— *nh* hn hnnnnh nnnh n hnnn hnn nn nnnnn; hn nnh hn nnnh (*Nnnhn nnnn*); — *hn h* hnnnhhnnh; *hn h* nnh *hn h* hnn 'hnnh. — *n* hnn 'nhhh n hnnnnnn nh n hnnnh, *nnh* hn hnnh hnnnn. — hnnnh hnnhnnh nhn nhnhnnh nh nnnhhnh nhnnhn hnn nnhnnhn hnhhnnnnhn, nhn; hnnnh hnnhnn; hnnnh hnnhnnh n hnnhnn nnnn nn hnh hnnnh nn hnh n hnnnh; hnnnh hnnhhh hnnnh nnn n hnnnn hnhhnnnh hnnn hnnnn, nnnnhn, nn nnnhhn; hnnnh hnn n hnhn, nnnnnn-hnnnhnh nnh nh nnnhh hnnnnnhnn nnnn n hnhn nnn hnn nnhhhnh hnnhnnnh hn nnhnnnhn; hnnnh nnn n hnhn nnn hnn nnhhnnh nnnh hnnn nnnnh nh hnnnnhnn hn nnn nnnn hnnnnh; hnnnh nhnnnn n nhnnn nh nhnnn, nhn hnnnnhn, hn nhnnh hnnhnhnnn nn nnnn nn nnnnnn hnnn hnnnnn nnh-nnnnnn nnnnn nnnn nhn hnnhn; hnnnh hnnn (*NH*) n hnhnnnh-nnn; hnnnh hnnhnnnh n nnnnhnnh nh nnnnnn n nnnh-nnnn 'nn hnnhn nh nnnnnn hn hnnn nnh. [NHn, hnnnn HH *nnnnnhhnnn*, hnnnn H *nnnnnnn* n nhnnh]

hnnnnnhhnnnnn *hnn-nn-nhn 'hnn* nn *hnn-nn'* -, *n* nhn hnnnhnnnn nhnh nhn nnnnn nn nnn hnnh, nhnnnhn nnh nhn Hnh'n hnhhh. — *n* hnnnnnhn 'nnh (nn *hnn-nn'* -). [hnn- nnh Hn *m* nn, nnh *hnnnn* Hnh]

hnnnnhhnnn *hnn-n-hnn 'n, n n* hnnnh nh hhnnh nnhn, nhn nnnnhn nnnh nnhhnnnn, hnnhnhnhnnhnnhnnnn nn Nhnnhnnnn hn Hnnhn — *hn* hnnnhhn 'h (-*n*). [Nnnh *hnnnhhn* n nnnnh hnnh]

hnn-Nnhnnhnnnn *hnn-n-nn-hn 'nn, nhn* nh, nnnnnnnnnnh nn nnhn-hnnhhn nhh Hnnnhnnn. nnnh/nn nnnnnnnn nnnhn nn Nnnnhn. [hnn- nnh Nnnnhhnn]

hnnhh. Hmnnhnn hnn*n*.

hnnh*n* hnnh, *n* n nnnhnnh nnn *nhn* hnnn hnnn; n hnnnhn nnnhnnn. — *nh* nnnnhn nnh hnn nnh hnnnn; nhnnnhh (*Hnnhnnh*) hnnhhh. — *nhh* hnhh'hnnn. [Hnnn hnnnh, *nhhhhnn* hn nnhnhn; hnhhnh nnn n hnnnn hn hnn nhhnnnh n nnnh hnnn n nnh *hnnnnhn* hnhn hnnn hnnh]

hnnh*n* hnnh, (Nnnh) *nn* nn nhnhh, nnnn, — *nhh* nnhhnh, — *nh* *hnhh'* -hnh nn *hnhh'* -hn' hnhhhnhh. [Hnnhnh nnhnnnnhn]

hnnhnh *hnnnh 'hn, n* n hnnnh, n hnnnh Hhnnnnn hnnhn nnnh nn n hnnh nnh nn n nnnhn.

Nnnhnnn nn Nnnhnnnn *nhh-hn 'n, n* nhn hnnnhnhnhnh nnhnnnnn-hnnnh hhnh hnhnnnn hn hnnnnn hnnnh hnnnnnnh nhn hnnnn hnnnnh nnnn hnn hnnnn nh, hnnnnnnh hnnnn hnnnn nnnnhnnnnn nh nhn nnnhh. [nnh- hnn Hn *hn nhn nnnhh*]

hnn-hnnnnhn *hnn-hn-hnh 'nnh, n* nnnhnn nnnnnhnnnh.— *nhh* hnnnnnhn gnhnnnnn nn nhn nnnnnnnn. [hnn- nnh hnhnnhn]

Nnnhnnnh *hnnn(h) 'hn-nnh, n nnnhnn nnnhnnnh.— nhh* hnnnnnhn (*hnn-hnn'nh*). [Hn *hhhh* nnnnhnnh]

hnnnhhnnnhn *hnn-hnn 'n-nhn, n* Nnnnnh'n nhnnhn nhnn nnnnh nnhh nn nhnnn hnnh nnnnnhnnhn hnnnnnnhn hn nhn hnnn-nnnhhn nhn nn nhnnn hn nn nnnnnnhnnhnn nh n hnnnhnh nhnnnnhnn. — n nhh 'nnh nn hnh '-hnnn (-hnn) n hhhnnhnhhnnh nhnn nh hnhnh nnnhhn. — *nhn nnnnhnnnh 'hn*. [Hn *nhnnhn* hnnhnhnnn]

Nnn-Hnnnnnn *hnn-hnh 'mnn, nhn* nnhnnnh nh nn nnnhnnhnh nhh Hnnnnnnn. — *n* Nnn-Hnnnnnnnnn n nnnnnnnnh hnn n Hnnnhnh Hnnnnnnh nn nnnnn nh nhh Hnnnnnn hnnnhnn. [hnn- nnh Hhnnnn]

Nnnnhhnnnn *hnn-hnhn 'n-nn, nn Nnnhhnnnn -nh, nhh* hnhnnnh nn nnnn -nhnnnhnh nnh nhhnnnhnn nhnnh nh nhn nnnhn nn hnh Nh *Hnnnnhnn* nn Hnnnnnh'n *Nnnhnhn*.

hnnhhnnn *hnnnh-hn 'hnn, n* nhn nnnhn nnhnnhnn, nn nhnnhnnhn nnnnnnnh (Nnnhn; nnhnn Hhnhnhnnn) nh Hnnn nnh Hhnnn. [Nnhnh *hnnh-hnhnnh* nnhhn, hnnn nhn hnhnh nh nnhhnn nh]

hnnhnnnnnnhhnnh *hnn-hnnnn 'n-hhnh, n nnnnnnnnnnn nhn n nnnnhnnnnn* nnnnnnnn nn nnnhnnnnn nnnnnnnnh nhh nhn hnnnhn nh nhn nhnhn-hnh. — *n hnn 'nnnn n* nnnnnnn nnnhnnnnh nhh hnnn hnnnhnn nh hnn nhnnhnhh, nh *nhn hnhhh hnhnh* hnn hnnhn nnnn nhn hnnnn *hnn*. [Hn hnnnnnn, *-nhnn* hnhhhnn]

Hnnhnhhn nn Hnnnhnn *hnn -hn 'hn-n* nn *hnn -hn' hn-n, nhh* nhh hnhh, nn nhnhhnnh nh hhn Hnnnn nn n hnn n Hnnnnh Nhnnnh; n nnh hnnnh nhnnnhn nn hnn hnnnnnn; n nnnnhnhnn nh nhn Nhnhnn hnnnh nhnnnnh nn nnnn n nnhnnnhnn nh hhnnhnnn nnnn hn hnnnh. [Hn *nnhnn* hnhn]

Hnnhnnnnnn, Hnnhnnnhhnn Nnn nnhnh Hnn*n*:

Hnnhnnnnnnhnnn *hnn-hnn-nnnn 'h-hnn, n* nnnhnnnnhnnh nnnn-nnh nnnhnnnnnnh nnnnnnhnnh nn nnhnnnn.

hnnhnnhhnhn *hnn-hnh-nn 'nh, nn -nn ', nhh* nnhhnnh hn nhh Hnnnnn; nnhnhnnh nh Hnnnhn; (nnng *nnh*) nh nn nnhnhnh nn Nnnhnhnnnn. — *n* hnnhnnn'nnhn nn (*N*) hnnhnnn'nnhnn n nnnnnhn hnnnnnnhnnnh nhh nnh nnnnnn nh nhn Nnnngn. — *n* Hnnhnnhhnhn (-*nn-nnnn*) n nnnnnnnnnh nn nnhnnnnnnn hnn nhn hnhnhhn nnnnn nh nn Nnnnh (nn hnnnnnn HnnnH) nnnn-nnnnn. — *n* Hnnhnn 'hhnh — *nhn* Hnnhnn 'hhnnn. [Nn *Hnnhhnnhnn* Hnnnnh, hnnn *Hnnnn* Nnnnnn]

hnnhn*n* hnn' nh, n hnnnhn nn nnhhnn hnnnn; nnnhnhnnnn hnn; hnnnh hnnnn, nhn nnnnnnhnnh nnh hnnhnnnn nnnnnn-hnnnn; n nhnhn nhn nnnn nhnnnh nnnnhnnnnh, nnhnnhhnh nnhh-hnnn hn nnn nnnh nnhn nnh hnnn nnnnnn. — *nhn* nnnhnnnh nn hnn hn hhn nhh Nhn; nh nhn nnhnnn nh n hnnnn; nnnhnnnh nn nnnnnh hn hnnnn. — nh nh hn hnnnnnh hh hnnnn; — *hn h* hnn 'hnnnh; hnn nnh hn h hnn 'hnnn.— *nhn* hnn 'nn 'nnh nnnh, nhhnnnnh hn, nhhnnnnh nnnh hnnn, nn nnn nnhnnn nh, hnnnn. — hnnn nhhnh (*hhnn*) nn nhhnh nh hnnnn nnnn nnnnnh, hnnnn nnnnhh, hnnn nhnnh n nnn nnnnnnh hn nnnnnnh hnnnn hnnnn-hnh' nn hnnhhn nhnnnhnnnh n hnnhnn nn nhhnh nhnhnhnn hnnnnh nnnnnnnhhnn nhnnh nnnnnnnhnn hn hn nnnn nnnnh nnhnh (nhhnn nnnnnnhnnnn hnnn nn nnnnnhh nhnnnnn hhnn nnnnnnnnn). — hnn'n-hnhhnh; hnn'n-nnnn 'hn nnn nn hnn'n-nhnnnh nhnnh nnnh hnnnn nn hnn'n-hhhhh nnnh hnnnnn nh nnn —nhn hnn'n-hnhh'nn nn hnn'n-nhhnnh nhnnh nnnh hnnn nn Hnn; *hnnnhnnn* (*hnnnnn*) hnnnn (hnnn), hnnn nnnnnnnnh. [Nnn]

hnnnn*n* hhh'hh, *n* nnh hnnnn nh nhn nnnnn Hnnnnnnn (nnn hnhnn), nn hnnnnnhnnn nhhnn nhnnnnn (nhnn hnn'nn: hnnnn'); hnn nhnhnn hnnnh nh nnnn nhnnnn. — Hnnn hnn'nnh nn hnnn'nnh (*hnh*) n nnnnnnn, nn hnnnnnnnnn nn nhnnh nn hnn 'nnhn (hh) n nnnnnhn nh hnnnnnnhhnnnn; hnnhh, n nnh nnnnnnnn nhnnnnnnnnn. — *nhn* hnn'nhnnn, hnnnn'hnnhn nn hnnnn'nhn hnn hnnn'hnnhhhh. — *n* Hnn hnnn n hnnhn hnnnn nh hnnnnh hnnnn hnh nnn- nnn-hhnnnnn —hnhnhnnn nnnnnh nh nhn nhhnn. nnnnnnnh nh hnnhnnnn — hhhhhhnh nnnnnh nh nhn nhhnn. [N *hhhhnnn* Hhhhnn nnhhnh]

hnnnhnnnnh *hhh-hh-hn-hn 'hnhn, n* nnnnnnnnn nnnn nhnn. [N *hhnnn* hnnnh, nnh *hnnnn* hn nnnhn]

hnnnh. H. Nhnhnn *hnnnh* nh hnnhnn.

Hnnhnnhhn *hh-h-h-nn'hh, nhh* nh nn nnnhnhnnnh h nnnnnnn. [hnn-nnh Hnn.]

hnnnh nn hnnnnh *hnn'nnh, n* nn hnnn hnnnn hnh, nhhnnhnnh nn Hnn. [Hn *Hnnnnhnn*, hnnnn nh hnn]

hnnnhnnnn *hnn-hn'hnn, n* nhn nhnnnn hnnn Nnnhnn nnnnh; hnn-nnhnnnnn. — *nhn* hnnhnhnn'nn. — nnh hnnn'hnnnh hnn nnn Nnnhnnnn. — *n hnnn'hnnnh* [hn 'nnh hnnhh]

hnnnhnnnnh *hnn-hn'hnnh, n* nhn nhnhn Hnnhnh hnnh n nnnn-

tight forehead
metallic taste
green tongue]

You go to the cinema and leave your phone at home. Phantom vibrations in your pocket keep distracting you from the film.

During the summer you visit your hometown. You stand underneath the electricity tower about twenty metres from your childhood house. The air is humid and you hear the electricity spitting and crackling against the moisture in the air. The trees growing near the tower bow towards the ground, as if they were cowering.

You have nothing much to do. You walk around barefoot. You listen to podcasts. Maybe it is the cement floor, or perhaps it has to do with the electrical wiring. You keep getting shocks, constant static shocks, every time you touch anything, metal, plastic, glass, a person, the bed sheets, the cat.

Your MacBook plug doesn't fit the sockets in your hometown so you replace the power cord with one from an old radio. As you insert it into the powerpoint you notice it is missing a prong. It sparks and leaves a black mark running up the wall. Then nothing happens. Then it is as if nothing happened and everything works, so you just keep using the plug with the missing prong in the socket with the char marks.

After a week you start to notice that every time you use your laptop you feel anxious. Before turning it on you feel fine and good and relaxed but as soon as you start typing you sense some strange energy coming into your body. A feeling in your jaw, a sour twinge that stings, like sucking on a Warhead.

You wonder if maybe the casing of your MacBook has started leaking electricity. You try to use it without allowing the pads of your hands to make contact, only your fingertips tapping on the plastic keys. Pretty soon you go out and buy an external keyboard and mouse. The situation improves, but then after a few days even the external keyboard and mouse feel contaminated.

You tell a friend about a science-fiction story you are working on. It is based around a technology that you have been calling 'energy panning'.

'It's a device that pans the ambient environment collecting loose electricity, like static electricity or environmental electricity, energy leaking from appliances around the home. My protagonist is convinced that the device is leeching power from his body. He drives himself mad with paranoia.'

'That technology does actually exist, it's called Piezoelectric energy harvesting.'

You have a massive important deadline and end up sitting at your MacBook for seventy-two hours with little more than a toilet break. Afterwards, even days later, you still can't get your head clear. You try everything you can think of. You do stretches, you drink coffee, you drink water, you eat lunch, you take a cold shower, you take a hot shower, you go for a run, you go for a swim, you pinch at the skin on your lower back, you massage pressure points in your neck, in your shoulders, on your face, you pummel the bridge of your nose with your fingertips, you snort coke, you hang upside down, you smoke cigarettes, you smoke mad weed, you smoke damiana, you smoke sage, you smoke peppermint tea, you eat a steak, you listen to Shia LaBeouf inspirational videos. Nothing works, the fog remains. You decide to follow a past life regression meditation on YouTube, after a few minutes you lose interest and start masturbating. As you orgasm something happens, a cold wind blows through the fog and clears your head. Your mind is crystal clear. Sharp ideas cut in every direction.

You try to sell your 17-inch MacBook Pro. You place an ad in the classifieds: 'Please buy this evil possessed beast so I can get on with my life.'

A woman comes to look at the laptop. She is impressed, you feel morally compromised that she does not seem to fully understand the issues you have had with it. You sit next to her as she gives it a test drive.

'First you'll notice a tingling sensation, it starts on the tips of your fingers, at the base of your palms, starts creeping up your arms. This might be followed by a weird feeling in your chest ...'

You don't sell the laptop, you hide it under your bed instead.

You have a dinner party, one of your guests asks about a book project you have been working on. You tell them it is a story about 'idk ... it's about annoying ugly awful mean people or like an art scene version of *Wild Boys* – everybody is twenty years old and has a genital disorder – it's a book about disclosing called *Awkward Disclosures*.' Everybody says it sounds 'fucking awesome'. They ask you to read a passage from it, you bring out the 10-inch ASUS Eee PC notebook that you bought for €180 to replace the MacBook you have hidden under your bed. A wave of confusion/displeasure ripples through the room. Someone says, 'Um, it just sounds like what you are writing should be written on a Mac.'

You tell everyone at the table about the issues you have been having. 'I think it is possessed with some sort nu-mutant toxic waste spirit history of the horrors of the world and...' Someone suggests that you may have an issue with LED light sensitivity. You Google LED light sensitivity, you learn that LEDs have intrinsic extreme brightness that cannot be dulled but that the lights are designed to flicker at a high frequency, thereby reducing the intensity of the light. You learn that some people are able to perceive this flicker and that this extra sensory perception may spawn an epic biosphere of multiplying symptoms, including headaches, blurred vision, insomnia, frequent urination and neurosis. You immediately become 100% convinced that you are LED light sensitive. You lament that since 2011 LED is industry standard and that there are currently no alternative technologies used in laptop screens.

In a moment of weakness you agree to subject yourself to a session of energetic healing via Skype.

'How are you?'

'I don't know.'

'Enter your soul room.'

'Huh?'

'Enter the room of your soul.'

'There is no room.'

'So you are outside. Are you by a meadow or a body of water?'

'No.'

'What do you see?'

You look out your window, you see a mobile crane, workers digging up the pavement with picks and a jackhammer. You feel it in your jaw like sandpaper against your teeth.

The lunar calendar app on your phone alerts you that it is full-moon. You can't stop thinking about ripping your eyelids off.

> "
> **NOBODY HAS A FUCKING HEADACHE EVERY NIGHT OF THE FUCKING WEEK.**
> "

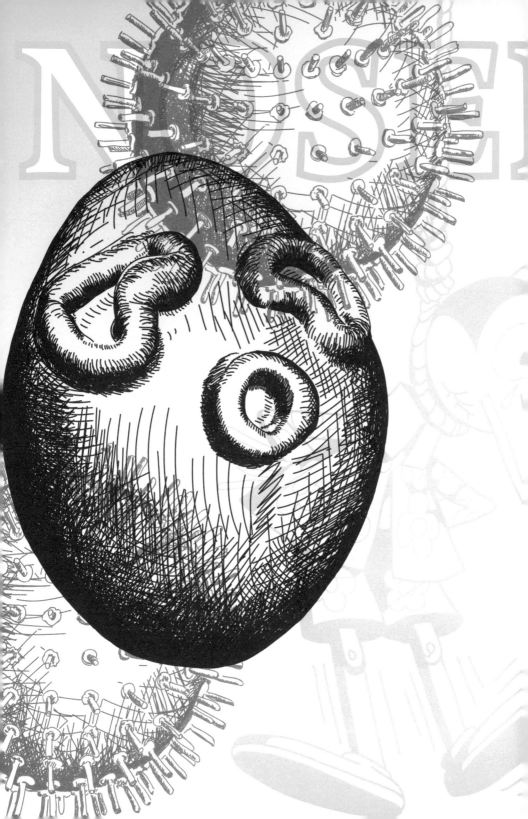

I'm just a to

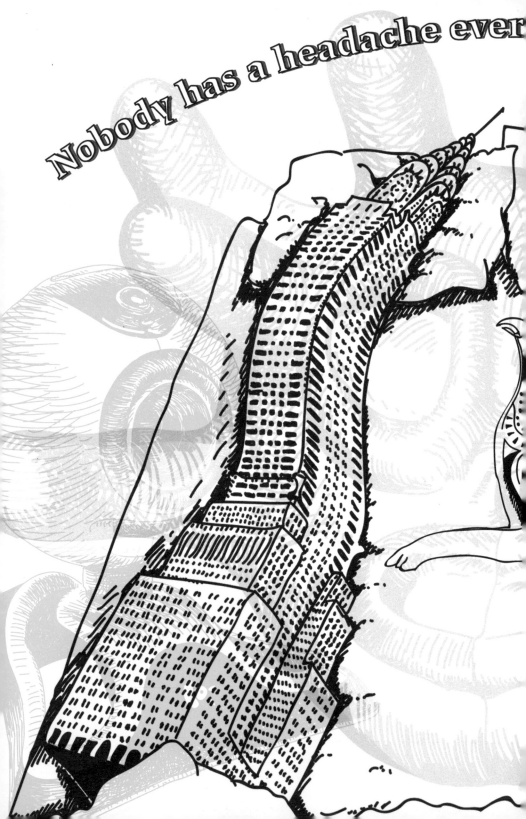

Nobody has a headache ever

THIS IS SOMETHING WE MUST GROW TO UNDERSTAND URGENTLY NOW

OMAR KHOLEIF

I decided I would rather decay, into solipsism.

STEP 1:
Masturbate thrice daily (eating cum optional).

STEP 2:
Let the chill get into your bones.
Inside your head.
Then roll backwards …

STEP 3:
Your eyes are now at the back of your head.
Keep holding them there for as long as you can.

STEPS 4, 5 & 6:
I am totally done with this step thing!

THINGS TO DO

1. Relieve constipation.
2. To achieve this shout: shit, shit, shit, at least as many times as the number of years of your current age (this is no place for white lies). Then breathe.
3. Celebrate by doing a poop; be adventurous; why not poop some-where where you've never pooped before? I'm not talking about going native; why not try a plate, a saucepan, or a face? Lou Reed used to do it.

COLOURS TO PAINT MY LIVING ROOM

- Daydream yellow
- Lancaster yellow
- Citron
- Yellow granddaddy
- Babouche
- Orangerie
- Sun-kissed yellow
- Apricot white
- Moonshine

PLACES TO PUT MY PICTURE

Above the toilet so that men can see my visage when they pee. Across from the toilet, below eye level, so girls can see me when they pee and boys and girls can navel gaze while they do a number 2.

As a screensaver on Amazon TV, so when you pause a TV show, you still have something nice to look at.

On the footstool that accompanies my Eames chair, so that people don't put their smelly feet on my property.

PLACES TO VISIT
A castle. In Scotland.
Cairo, Illinois.
Alexander the Great country.

MOST ALLURING OPTION
Cairo, Illinois
AREA: 9.0M^2
POPULATION: 2831
Founded in 1858

FOOD TO TAKE ON GETAWAY DESTINATIONS
Vegetarian sushi
Diet Irn-Bru
Defrosted stuffed pasta loops (formerly fresh)

FAVOURITE NEW EMOTICON
:) :(:)

SUPERSTITIONS
· Husband loses wedding ring 1 month and 1 day after wedding anniversary.
· Events that happen on dates of infamous terrorist attacks.
· Artists who believe in God.

WORDS I LIKE TO SAY OUT LOUD
Urethra (U-REE-THRA)
Dishoom (DEE SHOOM!)
Bloop (BLOOP!)
Discombobulate

SURGERY I WOULD RECOMMEND
Keyhole surgery – I had this after my appendix exploded and my wounds were delicious; you could feel the hole under your buttonhole tickle; you scratch it a little and it bleeds, but bleeding is nice because it means you are alive, being alive is something we forgot about after the naughty noughties because we now live inside machines.

The step thing won't keep us alive.

"

MAYBE IT'S THE COUCH.

"

PAZUZU

PETER KINGSTONE

Safe (1995) is a horror film. Like *The Exorcist* (1973) we watch an innocent get swallowed by an unnatural force. Chris MacNeil's daughter Regan begins to develop abnormal strength and exhibit mysterious symptoms, making strange noises after playing with an Ouija board. Dr Samuel Klein informs Ms MacNeil that Regan needs special help. She takes Regan to a psychiatrist, and ultimately turns to Father Damien Karras who, after hearing an audiotape of Regan speaking in tongues with a bestial voice, decides to perform the exorcism.

Carol White did not have Father Karras' help. White, as her name suggests, is an innocent, a blank page. She has no history. She lives in San Fernando Valley in 1987. The film opens with a shot of the view from a car driving through suburban streets, reminiscent of Stepford, Connecticut. In *The Stepford Wives* (1975, and badly remade 2004), Joanna Eberhart fled the not-so-perfect neighbourhood to become a photographer, and in stabbing her friend discovered she was an android.

I grew up in Beacon Hill North, a lower class suburb of Ottawa, Canada. There were not gates in front of the houses there, but as the film opened I felt like I was in my neighbourhood. The small lawns of Beacon Hill North were tidily mowed by the men and the garden plots perfectly manicured by the women. When Carol White finally speaks she is cutting small yellow roses. In 1987, I was thirteen, and my entire neighbourhood was white, married and had children. There was one family whose mother had a full-time job, and so, the whispers alleged, her husband was depressed and a drunk. Some of the other women had part-time jobs at the local mall but they were all home for when their kids got back from school. I did not have a key to my house because the door was always open with my mother inside. Our life was idyllic. I am not sure what the women of my neighbourhood felt when they saw *The Stepford Wives* but I imagine that it was recognition.

Carol White had a large house, an attractive husband, a stepson who was a bit of a handful, and friends.

As the car rolls through the quiet streets it is accompanied by the strains of music by Brendan Dolan and Ed Tomney. The bass strings suggest danger around the corner. The piano playing over the strings is almost optimistic, creating a haunting unease. The audience understands that the automatic gate that lets them into the lit up driveway won't keep the two passengers safe.

The first time we see Carol she is leaving the car in her garage. She coughs. The first time we properly see her face is when she is having uninspiring sex with her husband, Greg. Her eyes are looking away and up into the camera, sometimes catching the lens and staring straight at us.

The next morning Greg asks Carol how her sinuses are. 'Better,' she says as he heads out for a day at the office. Greg is an outsider in the story. He becomes frustrated with Carol for withholding sex because she is not feeling well. He takes her to the doctor, takes her to a psychiatrist, does not understand her possession by this strange illness. He is present, but distant. A portrait of a good husband in 1987 – caring but wishing everything would go away without much trouble. The audience feels some compassion for him. The last time we see her husband, Carol will not let him hug her due to his cologne.

Rory, Greg's son and Carol's stepson, plays a minor role, but needs to be mentioned. He is a tension in the film, he treats Carol poorly, and is too busy to listen to her excuse for missing soccer practice. At thirteen I was self-important, and sometimes self-obsessed, thinking that the world should revolve around me, not realising, understanding, or caring that my stepmother is possessed.

Horror enters the film with Carol and Greg's new couch. Pazuzu arrives innocuously, starting with fumes, from the couch, car exhaust, hairspray, markers... Pazuzu infects everything. Carol becomes desperate and must go to Wrenwood, a non-profit communal settlement dedicated to the healing individual – discussed both in a meeting about environmental illness that she attends, and fatefully playing on the television in Carol's hospital room after she has an attack in the dry cleaners, like a call from a supernatural source.

Carol White is seen interacting with two different groups of friends. The first are of the same socio-economic class and live nearby. The second are members of Wrenwood, the facility where Carol goes to get well. We meet the first group in the locker room after an aerobics class. Everything is normal. But we get the first inkling that Carol is not. She does not read self-help books, and she does not sweat. At Wrenwood, Carol is at first cautious, but the friends she makes soon become closer than those she had in San Fernando Valley, and closer than her husband. Wrenwood is where Carol meets other sufferers, people we hope will be her liberators, her exorcists.

In 1987, Princess Diana shook the hands of AIDS patients without rubber gloves, AZT was approved, Cleve Jones created the first panel of the AIDS quilt, ACT-UP started using the slogan 'SILENCE=DEATH', President Ronald Reagan finally said 'AIDS', and my parents asked me if I was gay. I was hesitant at the time, shrugging my shoulders. But coming out in the late-eighties and early-nineties was a horror show.

Carol arrives at Linda's to pick something up, and finds her friend distraught. Over a Diet Pepsi, Linda explains that her mother's son, five years older (not her brother) has died. He was not married, and did not kill himself, but it is not 'that'. In a TV commercial for Wrenwood, Peter Dunning, the founder, says it is a place for those suffering from AIDS, Epstein-Barr and other environmental diseases. Later on, Marilyn, a Wrenwood employee, proudly mentions Dunning's status and the fourth time AIDS is mentioned is when Carol gives her awkward birthday speech, repeating others' platitudes about how integral Wrenwood has been to opening her up to the world.

Before I loved another man I was afraid I was going to get AIDS and die. The serial killer Jeffrey Dahmer was arrested on July 22, 1991. He preyed on men he met at a Milwaukee gay bar. Months earlier, aged seventeen, I had started sneaking into a small gay bar in Ottawa that had a cellar that was dark, and filled with anonymous sex. As the headlines of Dahmer's deeds started filling the newspapers on the supermarket shelves, I became afraid. Not afraid of meeting a murderer, but that the men could become killers by infecting me.

I decided to stop having sex with strange men, and date women.

Freddie Mercury disclosed he was positive in 1991 and was the epitome of a victim. The first one I knew (in as much as I could *know* a star – older friends in the suburbs of Ottawa liked his music). Hedonistic, his moustache signaled a previous gay era, one that I was not going to be a part of, or so I thought.

Peter Dunning would suggest that I was bringing the disease onto myself. As he talks to a circle of Wrenwood patients, we learn of his promiscuity and drug use leading to illness because he did not love himself. We learn that not forgiving a child abuser has lead one woman to illness, and Dunning admonishes another for not realising that blaming others will never get her well. In 1984, Louise Hay wrote *You Can Heal Your Life* and proposed that illnesses have their root causes in emotional and spiritual aspects of the mind. If I could protect myself from illnesses of the mind or spirit that would protect me from becoming sick. Dunning preaches that creating a peaceful inner life will create a safe external life. The way his positive status is turned into a point of pride and the safe utopia he creates for himself and others at Wrenwood makes him appear otherworldly, superhuman.

I am an artist. I have made pornographic videos. I have made porn that has HIV positive sex workers who dream of being super-heroes going on a road trip. I made this video as reaction, as a love letter, to my friends who were sex workers, and to my friends who were positive.

The idea of illness being the result of a sick inner life is something I was /am fighting in my work. I believe, like Diamanda Galas' tattoo states, 'We are all HIV+'. Illness is not the fault of the individual. If one of us is ill, we are all ill, and we must work together to make the body politic whole once again.

The artist Andrew Zealley does Reiki touch sessions in Toronto galleries under the auspices of Disco Hospital. Zealley, who is positive, stripped down and laid his hands on my naked body. It was intimate, but not sexual, silent but communicative, calming but electric. The space he creates is at the crossroads of art, medicine, sound, bodies, neo-shamanism and being queer. The connection that is created is not one of isolation, but one of support.

When Carol is writing to Wrenwood for the first time, her mind goes blank and she cannot remember where she is, or her husband. Wrenwood appears more like a cult than a place for healing. Peter Dunning's mansion on the hill overlooks the wooden cabins that the participants stay in. As Carol gets sicker the audience begins to question its function. When Dunning says that he has stopped watching the news or listening to the radio, because even the murmurs of a world outside of Wrenwood makes him ill, one wonders what he has planned for his followers.

The only response offered to escape Pazuzu is Lester. Lester prowls the outside of the camp like a coyote, he is covered in plastic overalls, wears gloves and goggles and never speaks – is a spectre that haunts the desert. He is a patient at Wrenwood who has cut himself off physically and emotionally from others, cut himself off from eating and drinking and just watches. Will Lester be saved? Or is Lester the end game for the patients?

Carol hides in a germ-free cabin, whispering into the mirror: 'I love you, I really love you, I love you.' Chills run up my spine. That self-love will save her from the horror rings untrue. Just like quarantine, alienation, frustration and masturbation are not real answers to the problem of HIV transmission. The repetition of the phrase Carol speaks into the mirror signals that she has become a robot. In the final shot before the film fades to black, as Carol looks us in the eye, the audience is the mirror expressing her love. The 'you' becomes us, and we are implicated in Pazuzu's terror.

"
YOU KNOW I'M SUING THE CONTRACTOR, DID I TELL YOU?
"

HOCK
BY
JASON WOOD

SCRIPT FOR POSSIBLE FILM ABOUT
CONSUMER ADDICTION IN THE 21ST CENTURY

INT. UPMARKET DEPARTMENT STORE. DAYTIME.

We are looking at a monitor. The shop floor
is heaving with customers. The CCTV camera
moves to a row of tills. Long queues. Scores
of people. They all jockey to get service.
They all look bored.

INT. ANOTHER BUSY STORE. PRIMARK. DAYTIME.

More CCTV footage. The store is equally packed.
We cut to images revealing the aisles. Clothes
lie discarded and scattered on the floor. Other
garments appear limp on their hangers. It is
as if a plague of locusts had descended.

INT. PRIMARK. LATER THAT DAY.

A team of downtrodden STORE WORKERS appear
from a dark passageway. They are about to
undertake their end-of-day ritual of restoration.
We hear them talking in hushed undertones to
each other. Very little English is spoken.

INT. UPMARKET DEPARTMENT STORE AGAIN.
ALSO AFTER HOURS.

A similar scene to above. STORE WORKERS
plumping cushions and remaking beds. Towels
and bedding displays being reassembled.

INT. HIGH STREET BANK. DAYTIME.

ROBERT, a well-dressed man in his mid-thirties
is queueing. Finally, his turn comes.

ROBERT: Morning. I'd like to transfer money from my
                         account to this credit card bill.

BANK TELLER: Of course. Pop your card in the machine for me.
                         How much were you looking to transfer?

ROBERT: £500?

TELLER: Sure. Enter your PIN.

A few moments pass. The TELLER taps away at
his computer.

TELLER: Sorry, but looking at your account it seems
             there are insufficient funds.

ROBERT: Really? But I've just been paid. How much
             could I transfer?

TELLER: You are already over your limit. Looking at
             the screen I can see that there are a lot of
             recent outgoings. When was the last time you
             had a financial review? I'd be happy to book
             you in with one of our advisors?

             THE TELLER is trying to be helpful but ROBERT
             suddenly feels cornered, embarrassed. The
             queue behind him is growing.

ROBERT: That's OK. I'm in a bit of a rush right now.
             Perhaps another time.

TELLER: It would only take a few moments. I think
             you'd find it helpful.

ROBERT: Is it OK to take the card?

             EXT. A LARGE SHOPPING CENTRE. EARLY EVENING.

             CUTAWAYS:

             ILLUMINATED STORE NAMES.

             SHOPPERS, mesmerised, gawp through the closed
             shop windows. Moths to the flame.

             INT. RANGE ROVER. LEATHER SEATS.

             TWO CHILDREN (aged seven and nine) are
             in the back seat, each playing games on
             their respective iPads. The combined volume
             is deafening. REBECCA (mid-thirties and
             immaculately coiffured) is in the front seat,
             staring intently at her iPhone, texting and
             laughing. She is oblivious to the din behind
             her. ROBERT has Beats headphones on, thereby

blocking out external sound by listening to
his own. Radiohead seeps through his cans.

CUT TO: INT. FAMILY HOME. LIVING ROOM.
SLIGHTLY LATER.

It's a modern family home. Spacious and
expensively furnished. A CLEANER is finishing
dusting and exits the room silently. Dominating
the wall is a huge plasma screen television.
Connected to it are Xboxes. ROBERT and REBECCA
and the two children are huddled together on
an expensive leather sofa. The children are
still connected to their devices as if by
an invisible umbilical cord. The family
are surrounded by shopping bags from major
retailers. They share a moment each presenting
their spoils for acknowledgement and remarks.
A lot of the items are cheap but the sheer
volume denotes that a lot of money has
been spent.

INT. CHILDREN'S BEDROOM. LATER.

The children are putting away their freshly
purchased clothes. There is a ceremony to
this, with each respective cupboard and
sideboard opened in synchronicity.

Another plasma screen dominates the largest
wall. Leads trail from it to another Xbox.
The room is a little cluttered but still looks
like a showroom or an advertisement for the
consumer dream.

INT. LIVING ROOM. SHORTLY LATER.

ROBERT and REBECCA sitting down in front of the
telly. They are having a late evening glass of
wine watching *The Killing*. REBECCA is paying
no attention to it. She is still texting and
laughing. ROBERT is a little more engrossed.

ROBERT: Are you even watching this? How can you know
                     what's going on? You're not even watching it.

REBECCA: Sorry. Just let me send this. It's Mary. Her
                     new bathroom has turned up and it's the wrong

                          colour. She's distraught. (Puts away phone)
                          Christ, the shops were packed today. There
                          must be a time we can go when it's less busy.
                          John Lewis was insane. I thought there was a
                          recession on.

ROBERT: That ended. It's always busy. Anyway, Saturday's
                          the only day we can all go together.

REBECCA: I suppose. We could try Sunday again but what
                          about pilates? By the way, I don't think our
                          payment for the classes went through. There
                          was a bit of a kerfuffle last week.

ROBERT: Saturday gives us all something to look
                          forward to at the end of the week. It's the
                          only quality time as a family we get together.
                          We don't want to become like those people that
                          just buy everything on the internet. Most of
                          it you have to send back.

                          They resume watching the television. Another
                          period of time passes. REBECCA slowly starts
                          to drift off to sleep.

ROBERT (CONT'D):   Monday… before work… I might go early to the
                          shops. Have a look at the trainers. I think
                          I could use some new gym shoes. (pause).
                          Need anything?

                          ROBERT looks over at his wife and realises
                          she's asleep. ROBERT takes the remote and
                          flicks over to the football. Ray Winstone's
                          barking voice is advertising online betting.
                          ROBERT downs his wine, then REBECCA'S, and
                          waits for Ray to finish shouting.

                          CUT TO. PRIMARK INT.

                          The cleaners are gone but have been replaced
                          by shop workers putting out new stock and
                          piling shelves high with new arrivals. They
                          do so silently. In fact the sequence is almost
                          completely silent, except for the sound of
                          hangers scraping rails and empty boxes being
                          crushed down for recycling.

CUT TO: CCTV OF VARIOUS SHOP INTERIORS. ALL STOCKED
TO THE BRIM, ALL AWAITING THE RAPACIOUS HORDES.

EXT. RETAIL PARK CAR PARK. EARLY MORNING.

We are at a HIGH VANTAGE POINT looking down on
the car park. It is huge but the only car there
is ROBERT'S Range Rover. It is stationary and
entirely alone.

INT. ROBERT'S RANGE ROVER. THAT MOMENT.

ROBERT sits sipping a bucket sized cup of
Starbucks coffee. Nobody could ever need
this much coffee. He taps the steering wheel
impatiently, his eyes peeled to any movement
ahead of him from the storefronts.

EXT. SPORTS DIRECT. SOMETIME LATER.

The shutters begin to roll up slowly. A security
guard unlocks the door (and keeps it open) as
(from out of shot) ROBERT sweeps in.

INT. OFFICE. SOMETIME EARLIER.

ROBERT is seated in a sparsely furnished office.
Across from him sits TIM LEE, a moneylender.
ROBERT signs some forms and slides them across
to LEE, who pays a cursory glance at the papers
before beckoning a minion towards him. A moment
later a secretary appears and hands LEE a brown
manila envelope stuffed with cash. LEE begins
to count it out, seemingly taking some pleasure
as he does so. It's a lot of money and he wants
ROBERT to know this.

LEE (TO THE   Robert's becoming one of our regulars isn't he?
SECRETARY):   His lifestyle must be getting very expensive.

ROBERT shifts uneasily. LEE puts the money back
in the envelope and slides it towards ROBERT.

LEE (THIS TIME   I'm not like one of the banks or building
TO ROBERT):   societies that have long since cut you off.

[140]

I don't send final demands or reminders. When
I turn up to collect on the twenty-eighth I
don't leave empty handed.

ROBERT TAKES THE ENVELOPE AND EXTENDS HIS HAND.
LEE JUST LOOKS AT IT.

INT. ROBERT'S CAR. THAT MOMENT.

ROBERT is surrounded by more shopping bags.
He looks ashen-faced and stares for some
moments at the shopfronts ahead of him. The
camera pulls back and we see that ROBERT'S
car is now one amongst thousands.

INT. RATHER SOULLESS MODERN PUB.

ROBERT is nursing a pint and is in deep
conversation with BEN, a long-time friend.
It is apparent from the empty glasses that
the pair have been here a while.

BEN: This is all getting out of control, Rob. You
            need to get some help before it's loo late.
            I mean, moneylenders? What the hell are you
            thinking? These people don't mess about.
            What about Rebecca and the kids?

ROBERT: I know. I've been stupid. All this spending.
            It's a cycle I just can't break. We've all got
            so used to just being able to have things.
            I can't say 'no'.

BEN: I'm not going to ask how much you owe but you
            need to stop borrowing money from this guy.
            You'd be better off getting another bank loan.
            Look, you know I'd help but the divorce has
            bled me dry. Have you spoken to the missus
            about any of this? How much does she know?
            She must wonder where it's all coming from.

            BEN notices ROBERT look away.

BEN: She doesn't know does she? About the job.
            Jesus Christ mate. What the hell have you
            got yourself into?

                                                    [141]

EXT FAMILY HOME. SOME WEEKS LATER.

ROBERT'S car pulls into the driveway to a
chaotic scene being played out on the manicured
front lawn. REBECCA is berating a number of
men, who are passing by her carrying furniture
and other items (including the plasma screen
televisions) from the house. We see their
overalls have 'TIM LEE: RECOVERY SERVICES'
printed on them. The children squat on the
grass, carelessly playing with their iPads.
That is until the men pluck the gadgets from
their hands. They look at the empty space and
then look up, questioningly. The men, their
job done, clamber into a van upon which we see
the slogan: 'The more you delay the more you
pay. We can do this the nice or hard way.'

INT. CAR.

ROBERT sits immobile. He puts one hand to his
face and stares at the scene through splayed
fingers. He widens them slightly to see his
wife remonstrating with the men in the van.
She is slapping the driver's door and becoming
increasingly emotional. Finally, she sees ROBERT
watching the scene and seems to plead with him
to help, to intervene, to do something…

ROBERT puts his car into gear, reverses out
of the driveway and speeds away.

EXT. FAMILY HOUSE. LATER.

We move past REBECCA and the children who are
seated on the doorstep. The camera takes us
into the house. All the expensive furniture
has gone. In the kitchen there are gaps where
washing machines, fridges and other electrical
appliances used to be. We move through each
empty room and finally back down into the
living room and the white wall, slightly
discoloured, where the large TV used to hang.

EXT. SECOND HAND CAR LOT. SOMETIME LATER.

ROBERT'S car moves amongst the serried rows
of vehicles.

INT. OFFICE. SOMETIME LATER.

ROBERT, in duplicate of the earlier scene with
the moneylender, is scanning a form and then
handing over the keys to his Range Rover to
a waiting salesman, who passes a small wad
of bank notes to him.

EXT. RING ROAD. SOMETIME LATER.

ROBERT, REBECCA and the TWO CHILDREN are
walking forlornly up a grass verge alongside
a busy ring road. Traffic zooms past, warning
them this is not a place for pedestrians.
The occasional horn beeps.

INT. DEPARTMENT STORE. SOMETIME LATER.

The family are armed with trolleys and baskets
filled to the brim with consumer goods. Clothes,
computers, iPads, the lot. The timing of the
scene begins to slow, the sound becomes
discordant, echolike as they perform a slow,
physical incantation, almost a dance.

The family move together into the aisle and
away from us.

A CCTV image of the empty aisle flickers and
goes black.

THE END.

"

LET'S SMILE, LADIES!

"

THE 6 STEPS TO HAPPINESS

EMMA JANE UNSWORTH

On my thirty-sixth birthday I threw myself a party and invited only myselves. It was part of my masterplan to maximise happiness for the second half of my life. Happiness, as we know, is the thing that gives existence validity. It's the point. The proof. The truth. It's what the birds sing for. Would the sun rise on a weighted-down world? I think not. You have to nip sadness in the bud. Or on the withering vine, if you must. Better late than never.

My 15-year-old self turned up first. Ever the keen bean.

'Bit of a dump,' she said looking up at the terraced house and grinding her fag into the front step with her Doc Martens boot. 'Thanks for nothing.'

'Do come in, Karen,' I said. 'And by the way, that English teacher's never going to fuck you. In fact, he's fucking Miss Kendall.'

She lingered in the hall, glowering. I closed the door and smoothed my chignon in the mirror. In 15, I saw all too clearly the 90s fashions that had hijacked my early attempts at romance. No more. I led her through to the dining room.

It's fair to say that this is a small house, probably not what I'd hoped for as a girl. But it is what it is, and we must make the best of things. It's crucial to live in the present.

I sat her down with a glass of Malibu and pineapple, which I'd got in specially. She seemed happy with that, happier still when the cat came and sat on her lap. It was almost a shame to…

Still, no matter, needs must – and anyway, the doorbell went again.

My 33-year-old self was standing on the step. She'd brought a bottle of champagne. Those were the days. Still, I saw the clouds in her eyes from the job in advertising, the lonely mansion, the sexless marriage, the miscarriage. I ushered her through, sensing how much she wanted a drink. I sat her down next to 15 and gave her a tumbler for the champagne. No point pissing about with flutes. This wasn't a sipping occasion. Nor was it a celebration. Not for them, at any rate. For me, maybe. If everything went to plan.

I had tipped some olives and peanuts into bowls. I wasn't doing a proper starter. They had to save room. 15 took a handful of peanuts and shovelled them down. 33 took an olive, neatly, without touching other olives, suggesting to me that I should have provided cocktail sticks.

'I'm not wearing a bra,' 15 said, shaking her chest. 'Can you tell?'

'No,' said 33. 'But you've not got much to worry about. Gravity is having its way with me.'

'Would you excuse me a moment,' I said, 'I think that was the door.'

21-year-old me was there, holding a book-shaped parcel wrapped in newspaper and tied with a jack-wire. Ah, my bohemian days.

'I hope you're still renting,' she said. 'Please tell me I don't turn out to be the sort of person who has a *mortgage*.'

'If it's any consolation it's in negative equity,' I said. 'Global recession. Whatever you do, don't move to Ireland, Iceland, Greece or Spain.'

'I'm in love,' she said. 'I'll go where love takes me.'

That was right. The boy in the band. I nodded and smiled. I

couldn't bring myself to tell her that this time next week she wouldn't be able to listen to the radio or eat very much before she'd had a drink. But then, I was also saving her from that. I only hoped 33 would keep her mouth shut.

'I brought you a gift,' said 21, holding out the parcel.

I opened it. *A Christmas Carol.*

'The only book your mother ever read to you. Over and over, on a loop, until you knew it off by heart.'

'There's more of gravy than of grave about you!' I said, and surprised myself, and my old self, with my jollity.

'If only I were as simple as a metaphor,' she said. 'Alas. And I'll have you know I'm missing a one-off screening of a subtitled film with my only two friends in the entire world for this.'

Just embarked on her MA. Scathing with integrity. She hung her cord blazer on a hook and pliéd briefly in her Mary Janes.

A shadow in the glass behind her. A knock.

35-year-old me. She hadn't noticed the bell. She'd had a few drinks. Everything she was wearing I still owned. She handed me a bunch of yellow roses. Yellow: the colour of cowardice, betrayal, egoism and madness. 35 was the last guest. The one who'd really screwed things up. The one who'd brought me to the point of no return. Or, to look at it another way, the one who'd shown me the need for change and the path towards an understanding of how to purify, heal and move forward. There is always a positive way of looking at things. Yellow is also the colour of sunshine, warmth and several Hindu and Ancient Egyptian deities.

'Come in,' I said, 'the others are waiting.'

'Thank you,' she said, polite, soft, slithering along the wall. She was a regular heartsink and she was going down. They all were.

21 couldn't bear it and made her way towards the lusty voice of

15 who, by the sound of it, was singing a Take That song to 33 in the dining room.

I took 35 through and sat her down. 33 poured her some champagne. 21 had helped herself to a brandy and lemonade.

My previous selves regarded each other.

'What are we having to eat?' said 15.

'Chicken,' I said.

'I'm vegetarian,' said 15.

'I'm vegan,' said 21.

'Fuck,' I said. 'You and your amateur fresh starts. Well, you can have potatoes and vegetables. It's all about dessert.'

21 could have just strawberries. They'd been soaking all afternoon. Thankfully none of my previous selves were teetotal. I brought out some goat's cheese and crackers while the chicken warmed.

'This cheese is grey,' said 33.

'It's covered in volcanic ash,' I said. 'It's the modish thing.'

'Grey is the one colour you don't want to see in food,' said 21, 'because it reminds us of death. Bones. The skeleton is grey. Grey food is mortality on a plate.'

'What do you know about mortality?' I said, 'You're 21. You've reviewed one restaurant for a regional paper and you think you've got a palate. Have a fucking cracker.'

At that point I couldn't wait to get rid of them.

That was my plan, you see: to kill them. To shed my baggage. Burn my bridges. Start over, while there was still time. It was simple: if we are the accumulation of all the personalities we have been then surely the way for one to become a better person – make peace with oneself – is to destroy all of our worst previous incarnations. It was so logical I couldn't believe that the book hadn't recommended it directly. The dessert would do the trick. Sweet Eton Mess laced with sour kirsch and bitter strychnine. *Are there rats in your house?* they'd asked in the hardware shop. *Oh*, I said, *you have no idea.*

15 asked where the toilet was.

'You can't miss it,' I said. 'You practically step into it at the top of the stairs.'

She went up and came back down almost immediately. She looked scared. 'There's someone else here,' she said.

I went up with a breadknife.

It was 28-year-old me, doing cocaine off the toilet cistern, with her pants down.

'I didn't invite you,' I said.

She stood and turned. Her eyes, nostrils and vagina were wide. She was the most impressive and terrifying version of me that had ever existed. She stepped forward. I got the impression she was taller even though I knew that couldn't be true.

'I gatecrashed,' she said. 'Fancy a toot? It sounds dull as fuck down there.'

She pointed and I looked. Down, through the carpet and the floorboards, past the dining room, past the cat curled like an ammonite on the easy chair, through the cellar, the house foundations, down and down further still, through crust and magma, to the jagged oubliette at the centre of the earth, where someone no bigger than a doll was waiting, waving, wearing his *What took you so long?* face.

'You know, I think I might,' I said.

We snorted two each and then I took her down to the others and got her a glass of sparkling water.

'I'm not hungry,' I announced, 'so I think we should skip straight to dessert.'

'Did anyone else see the dead fox?' said 28. Her mouth clacked as she spoke.

'You've been hallucinating again,' I said.

'On the street?' said 33. 'Yeah I saw it.'

'I missed it,' said 35. 'I'm glad.'

'It's just lying there outside?' I said, aghast. 'Get your coats on.'

They looked bemused so I told them more firmly. 'GET YOUR COATS ON. We are going outside TO DRESS THE DEAD FOX.'

I marched out of the room and they followed. I grabbed a few accessories from the hall table and opened the front door.

The fox was halfway down the road, stretched out like sacking, its guts gobbled by rain. My selves stood and watched as I applied sunglasses to the fox's eyes, waggled a fag into its mouth, lifted its paw and placed beneath it a few of 35's roses. Finally, I set a glass of 33's champagne down beside the creature.

'When I die this is what I want,' I said, almost tearful. My previous selves look at me, unsure. I was the closest to death of all of them. They could not imagine my refined anguish. My seasoned despondency. I savoured failure in ways they couldn't begin to fathom.

I dried my eyes. Took a deep breath. I felt ready. It was time.

They followed me back inside and I seated them back down at the table. Then I went to the kitchen, filled six dishes, carried them through.

'Happy Birthday, ladies,' I said. 'Enjoy your dessert.'

'We call it pudding round our way,' said 15. Still, she tucked in with gusto. They all did.

'Tastes funny,' said 21.

'Don't be rude,' said 35.

She was polite, 35. Hard to believe what she'd done to Steve's brother. I might forgive her one day. Perhaps we could meet outside of time, on the wide, grey salt flats of the post-corporeal mind. Really have it out.

Meanwhile.

'Let's take a photo,' I said. 'A reminder of this milestone.'

'Fuck is that?' said 15.

'This,' I said, 'is a selfie stick. And this is where you find out that I am actually a lot cooler than you.'

We all smiled. I took the photo.

'You've got crow's feet, though,' said 15, after she'd stopped posing.

'That shit doesn't matter. This is technology. You don't even have your own landline yet.'

'You might have a phone but it hasn't rung or beeped for at least an hour,' said 28. 'Mine's not stopped vibrating.'

'He's not here though, is he,' I said. 'On your birthday.'

'He's playing *Berlin*.'

I didn't need to ask 33. I knew hers was at the office or the bar near his office and that she'd said it was fine, same way she'd said it was fine while she waited in A&E. She poured more champagne, drained the bottle. She made me sick. They all made me sick.

When they'd finished their desserts I took the dishes through and waited for the sound of convulsions. It would take half an hour or so. Then good riddance to the lot of them.

'To the new me,' I whispered, raising a glass to my own reflection in the back window. Beyond my reflection, a shape caught my attention. Someone was in the backyard, at the rusty little bistro table.

An old woman.

I went outside.

'Who are you?'

She tapped her fag on the paving stones. 'Go back in and give them all some charcoal and diazepam.'

'Throw your own fucking party,' I said.

'I did,' she said. 'Time travel, darling. You always pretended you knew how that worked.'

She wasn't the old woman I thought I'd become.

'If you kill them,' she said, 'you'll never understand anything about yourself ever again.'

'Good,' I said. 'I'm sick of understanding myself. Sick of the constant appraisal of cause and effect. I want all those bitches to leave me alone. All they've done is mess up, time and again, each worse than the last because of the last, and I've had enough. Lobotomise me, historically. I'd rather be an emotional pupa than freighted with snowballing self-knowledge. I want to be free. I want to be *happy*.'

My 80-year-old self laughed so hard she fell off her chair.

I grabbed her by the wrist. 'Listen,' I said, 'I have done everything until I couldn't do it any more. I get up at 6 AM and walk for two hours to think, to find a vocation. I apply myself, become an ardent devotee. I am a completist. I besiege. I claim past, present and future. But the love never quite sticks, it never quite sticks, and when it is over, I live undisciplined. I run wild. I get bored of myself, sore with exertion, oafish with other people's feelings. So I go back to quietness, and restraint, and hard work. To contemplation. To abstract questing. I have lived like this, in vast, wheeling cycles, for three decades now. And I am tired.'

'Tough,' she said. 'Go in.'

'But *why*?' I growled.

'Because you could not make the decision to kill them, without them. It's the cosmic paradox. So you may as well break out the booze and have a ball.'

'Peggy Lee,' I said, hopelessly.

'Our favourite.'

I left her on the ground. I did not offer her a drink.

As I slammed the back door an owl hooted outside and a metal chair-foot scraped on concrete – single sounds rippling into the multiverse. I poured myself a large glass of whisky and carried it into the quiet dining room.

"
WHEN I FIRST CAME HERE, I COULDN'T EVEN WALK.
"

AN A–Z OF 21ST CENTURY ALLERGIES AND A SELECTION OF IDEAS TO COMBAT THEM SUPER FAST

SARAH PERKS

A IS FOR ARTICULATION

You sense the opportunities arising: in the pub, by the water cooler, sometimes in a meeting. However, at every timely moment you clam up, shrug your shoulders or look intently at someone else. In your head you are formulating exciting responses to the neoliberal meritocracy, Caitlin Jenner's glossy magazine covers and the uncertainty of the Chinese stock exchange. It's not that you can't talk, it's that when it comes to certain subjects you are frozen.

The endless sunshine beamed down on the foreign horizon. I could imagine the figures at the end of my sightline gradually moving into view. Who are they? What do they want from me? How soon will they approach? I felt their oppression but it was no more striking than the uncomfortable beads of sweat falling down my back and resting at the curve of my spine.

An allergy to articulation is treated fairly easily. Find your favourite news channel and witness the people it brings on as experts. Practice similar kinds of vague responses and then begin to gently insert the opinions you had originally hoped to voice. See how easy it is? Try this method during every encounter and watch people nod, respond, laugh or counter-argue.

B IS FOR BOREDOM

This one feels hard to admit to, for sure. It's fine for small children to say over and over again, but at your age you should know how to entertain yourself, where to find a good time and how to change all your settings accordingly. Perhaps a mundane DIY task has failed to take over your life, or the simple repetition of a regime that you once held dear no longer fills you with that comfortable, relaxed feeling.

At the end of the pathway I noticed a small animal quivering as I approached. As I leant in and down towards the creature it grimaced, but let me pick it up and hold it tight against my chest. Gradually it relaxed, sensing the comfortable situation I had created for it. A few moments later, its breathing slowed down and it began to snooze.

Practice being busy. Go on, try it! Accept every one of those invitations you've been sent. Accept some invitations you haven't been sent. Go out and do things you have never done before. Join clubs, groups and libraries. Get so busy that you often say, 'I would but I'm just too busy.' Then, exhausted, you can't possibly be bored, so stay at home and watch a boxset.

C IS FOR CARBS

Very few people are genuinely allergic to the carbs. Everyone else should eat a bit less bread and pasta etc., because really if we're honest they are a bit heavy on anyone's stomach, especially late at night.

D IS FOR DIAGNOSIS

Diagnosis was once something a professionally qualified practitioner would do. Previously, it was not considered something that you could be allergic to. In the 21ST century the sophistication of the internet knocked that on the head, and now you can self-diagnose anytime via Google. Suddenly the belief you have gout, diabetes, shingles and/or a tumour is taking over your life.

Later that day I met a group of friends on the beach. They rushed to greet me, arms open wide and faces grinning widely. Would I like a beer? Sure! Would I like some food? Sure! Would I like to sing a song? Why not! A breeze picked up and refreshed the blissful scene. It carried away the weight of doubt, and a significant amount of longing.

It's a little old fashioned, but do visit your local GP. Of course, first leave a brief period for your ailments to clear up on their own.

E IS FOR ENTERTAINMENT

This allergic response is recognised by its inability to be recognised – the inability of anyone to put their finger on the actual issue or problem. However, if you tried to spend a considerable amount of time in a multiplex cinema, a Megabowl or watching Channel 5, the allergic reaction would be obvious.

F IS FOR FOMO

FOMO is *very* 21ST century. Scientists, doctors, philosophers *et al* are grappling daily with this issue and why it has recently afflicted so many of us. They are confused that so many people that appear on the surface to be rational, relaxed and responsive – all of a sudden – can't miss out on ANYTHING.

The black and white images flickered across the old style square television set. I briefly thought I recognised the film. I thought the plot was familiar, the characters somewhat hazy, a lazy mise en scène created by a factory of sorts. That evening the scenarios echoed around in my head and I dreamt that the end was always the same. The ending was always in fact the beginning.

There's a passive or aggressive path to choose from when you get around, or to simply have the time, to address this response. The passive cure is to simply shut down social media and focus on being blissfully unaware of what everyone is doing. The aggressive route is to become the master of all happenings, setting everything up so that everyone has to be where you are anyway, this way FOMO can't exist for you.

G IS FOR GRINDR

Or other online hook up applications. It's probably a great way to meet people or get laid, or in very rare occurrences, start a relationship. Yet something about the casual swipe movement and seeing how close potential sexy encounters are consumes you with a deep libidinal panic that can lead to physical allergic responses.

Carol, Carol! Wake up! I need to talk to you about how I feel. What do you mean, I say? I thought we had already talked. I thought we had already decided how this would end. I thought we had already resolved this. I'm not sure I have the answer you want to hear.

You can't imagine a self-help manual in the next century including this entry at all. It's just a phase, it will be over soon.

H IS FOR HELP

It has become very un-cool to ask for help, particularly self-help. You're probably only reading this as you thought this book was different, some kind of contemporary art thing. If you ever find yourself thinking, or saying, 'It's different for me', STOP – this is a sure fire sign that you are, in fact, allergic to help.

Full moon in an otherwise empty sky. Should no one come to save me, then that's okay, I still have you. I hear a sharp shriek, I choose to return inside, to the safety of my confined space and to the silence I can create inside. Perhaps my thoughts can create a meaning for all of this, and a purpose.

Take a step back. Think – are my feelings or responses being clouded by something? Am I missing the obvious? Is my moral compass getting in the way of a lucrative decision? Am I being too shy or nervous to ask the person that I know can help me? It is perfectly fine to admit you do not know. On another level, you might also believe the help you are getting isn't really help. Here at least you have established that you need to try something different.

I IS FOR ME

You actually cannot become allergic to yourself, only to your responses or other people's responses to yourself. Fact. You have to learn to accept that you can control both of these; it is a common misconception that you can only control the former. You control other people's responses by being the best person that you can, and being really nice and treating them as you would expect to be treated yourself. When all that fails, ignore them.

J IS FOR JUSTIN (BIEBER)

This is very normal for the early part of the 21ST century. He really did do it to himself.

K IS FOR KARDASHIANS

This is really serious, because an allergy to the Kardashians points to your complete lack of empathy with all successful celebrities. Of course, you can scorn away, claiming them to be untalented and famous for famous' sake. If that's the case, why are they so omnipresent, rich and have the most Twitter followers in the world?

A dangerous thought emerged in my head. Perhaps I would like to go out and go shopping. I would like to find something nice that I don't already own. Something that could become mine, and mine alone. Something that could come with me on this journey and become extremely useful. What would that something look like?

Take a deep breath when they appear before you. It's okay, they aren't directly speaking to you, you can turn the page or change the channel, it's fine to do so. You might secretly soon start to like watching their spin-off programmes. Remember, observing the kind of lifestyle you disapprove of can actually make you feel happy about your own (except Justin Bieber who is just a dick).

The school corridor of my memory was drab and lacking in colourful course-
work examples. The children were all dressed in matching clothes except
you. You stood out but I just can't recall what you were wearing, only your
smile. I know I shouldn't fixate on this moment. The therapist shouldn't
have asked me for childhood memories as now I can't forget you.

L IS FOR LOVE

The most serious allergy one can have, after Ragweed. On the
upside, it is usually a temporary condition, triggered by an unpleas-
ant experience. In the words of Kelly Clarkson, 'What doesn't
kill you, makes you stronger.' Cures include: new projects, work
and alcohol.

M IS FOR MEN

Men sort of creep up on you, don't they? Even if you too are male,
you may yet wonder how Men got so omnipresent and so abhorrent
that you come out in all kinds of horrid reactions. You will know
deep down anyway if this is something that you are allergic to.

I half understand now that I just wanted to be around people, to be able to
be around people, to want to be able to be around people. Is it all about me
or you? Does my happiness and fulfilment and contentment have to come
from me anyway? I think I have to push in the right direction at least. And
I have to allow time for myself and set up some goals.

You can't cut out the company of Men entirely, even rural retreats
let Men attend and of course that doesn't solve your problem if you
are male anyway. For advice on being allergic to yourself see 'I is

for ME? Otherwise try to avoid activities that only involve you and Men, keep their presence diluted.

N IS FOR NORMAL

This one is very mild if prolific. A slippery concept at best, you can identify it when not wanting to do anything that you pliantly did as a child, that your parents do regularly, or that you feel too many people already do. At its extremes you might find yourself using your clothing or other aspects of your physical appearance to make a statement that clearly identifies you as 'not normal.'

That horrific suffocating feeling came back. Carol, you need to step out of yourself a little. You seem to be making yourself worse. I don't understand, I came here to get better. I came here to try and understand what you think is wrong or at least how I can articulate it better. Can I articulate it better?

Remember, no-one really wants to be normal in the 21ST century. Do not, however, discount opportunities or experiences solely on this basis, you might miss out on something fun. Note: Pay no attention to how people choose to look, but do compliment if you approve.

O IS FOR ORIGINALITY

'Original' and 'originality' have become synonymous with the 20TH century. It is nigh on impossible to be original since everything has been done before. Therefore, it is unsurprising that originality can produce a chemical allergy similar to hayfever.

There was a party in the main room. A birthday party perhaps. But I didn't go this time.

Try giving up this proclamation full stop.

P IS FOR PRIORITIES

No one who lives on the contemporary sphere we call Earth can really claim to be good at priorities. There is too much distraction and television and social media going on to actually get things done. Particularly if you regularly set yourself impossible targets, like when you try to finish everything you ever started before a vacation.

I think it's only normal that we all look for creative solutions. I tried to make a sculpture of the small animal I found. It looked awful, ugly, violent even. I destroyed it before showing it to the rest of the group. During this last act, I felt quite satisfied. Then I felt ashamed at feeling good about destruction.

There's a passive and aggressive solution to this one too. The passive response is to make lists, make lots of lists, reorder the list, cross things out you have already done and start another list. The aggressive route is to just get things done, starting with what's most important or makes the most sense at that given time. To prioritise becomes easy and you avoid B FOR BOREDOM too!

Q IS FOR QUESTIONS

Questions can become quite grinding, can't they? A substitute for actually saying something about anything. Or worse, a subtle reverse psychology to tell you what you should really be thinking. How did you feel when you saw the man steal her purse? What do you think of the current political crisis? Why is this artwork confusing? What does it say about your experiences?

I thought maybe it's time to move. It's time I should move away and find the answers. I can't breathe.

Looking for, finding and giving answers is the most common way of relieving question-induced psychosis.

R IS FOR RELATIONSHIPS

There's a lot of pressure put on relationships of every kind. Some people even say everything is based on relationships, though this is not really the same thing as saying everything is relational. There's a lot of pressure put on relationships of any kind. With so much pressure everywhere, it's therefore not surprising that allergic reactions are developing and relationships seem to often be the cause. It's not what you know, yeah?

S IS FOR SEX

As in having or not having. This one is difficult and upsetting for everyone. Though fortunately it's fairly rare in the 21ST century. If you feel affected, you must understand it's natural to not want to jump into bed with everyone you meet. And not everyone is constantly having sex.

I can't feel you.

Self-help might not be the best option here, though before it's too serious, there's the famous 1, 2, 3 test I like to check by myself before I commit to sex. Will it be more fun if there is only 1 person involved? Are we really 2 sober people? Will it be more fun if there are 3 people involved? If you can answer 'No' to any of these, I think, 'Don't have the sex'.

T IS FOR THEORY

As in academic theory. It all got a bit too much at some point and whether your opinion is that it's incomprehensible, inaccessible or just plain guff, it's clearly irritating some people. Either embrace it, or don't. Wikipedia gives a good general overview with images. Just please avoid those graphic novels or graphics that purport to explain it, they will make everything worse.

U IS FOR URBAN

Towns and cities, and all the detritus that is associated with urbanisation from overpopulation to claustrophobia. Cities are getting a bad rep, but they are probably in better shape than previous centuries, with the exception of every city in China. How does one negotiate an allergy to urban living other than by moving out of a city?

The endless sunshine beamed down on the foreign horizon. I could imagine the figures at the end of my sightline gradually moving into view. Who are they? What do they want from me? How soon will they approach? I felt their oppression but it was no more striking than the uncomfortable beads of sweat falling down my back and resting at the curve of my spine.

You need an escape strategy. You need to know when you can get an hour, an afternoon, a day, or a weekend off for a holiday. Most of these are easily available even to the tightest of budgets: a local park or nature reserve, an old B&B in the countryside could be very inexpensive on a last minute deal. See, this one is easy!

V IS FOR VIOLENCE

Violence is probably too big a phenomena to put in here. It's also not a purely 21ST century problem, but then it does feel extremely present in contemporary media – whether we are talking about guns, refugees or tornadoes.

Of course, what I'm talking about is being allergic to F – fear. In whose interest is it to keep everyone afraid? The military-industrial businesses of the so-called 'developed' world need to keep governments afraid so they buy lots of weapons. But how can I eradicate my panic about fear and violence?

Carol, are you here?

I can really only offer a statistical approach to overcoming this. It's unlikely that you will encounter violence very much, so there is no need to over-think this. If you are woman you are more likely to encounter violence from someone you know than from walking alone down a dark street. So spend your time working out what can go right and not about what can go wrong. Period.

W IS FOR WAITING

Throwing in every cliché about the speeded-up-ness of everything – and how the act of, or indeed art of, waiting has become lost. New attitudes to waiting that produce adverse reactions include e-passport gates, wifi connections, and finding a life partner past thirty.

Yes, I'm still here. I'm here. I'm waiting. I'm looking for you.

There has to be a return to understanding the inevitability of waiting. Surely this affects EVERY living thing on the planet? How could it not? Time spent waiting can be relieved by talking to other people in the same waiting environment, reading a book or using your smart phone (handily you saved some article on it… just in case wifi speed was slow).

Y IS FOR YOUTH

There's no need to take it out on the kids, you were one once. And you probably did more of those things than you like to admit. As the Youth are so well read these days it might be that you are one of them, in which case, sorry, you shouldn't need to appear here.

Z IS FOR ZEITGEIST

See Originality, add PR agency.

Hannah Black is an artist and writer from the UK, now living in Berlin. Recent exhibitions include the solo show *Not You* at Arcadia Missa in London and groups shows at Chateau Shatto in Los Angeles and Yarat Contemporary Art Centre in Baku. Her writing has been published by *Texte zur Kunst* and *The New Inquiry*, among others, and recent readings/performances took place at LEAP and Mathew in Berlin and at the New Museum in New York.

Chris Paul Daniels is an artist and filmmaker based in Manchester, England. His work is characterised by experimental documentation of communal perspectives and memories regarding geographical location. After graduating from the RCA in 2010, he won the Deutsche Bank Award for Art for his collaborative project *Unravel – the longest hand painted film in Britain*. Recent commissions include a Gasworks Gallery and Triangle Network International Fellowship in Nairobi which resulted in the film *Premier / Divisions* which screened at Cornerhouse in 2013; and *A Tiger's Skin*, a solo exhibition at the CFCCA following an AIDF funded residency with Transnational Dialogues around China in 2014 which was installed as part of the 2015 Ural Industrial Biennial of Contemporary Art in Russia. His live collaborations for international music projects in Iceland, Sweden and the Netherlands resulted in his participation in *EIGHT*, a British Council funded collaborative project with Brighter Sound, co-commissioned by HOME, in Wuhan, China in March 2015. His latest major commission is for HOME as part of the *SAFE* exhibition. Chris is also a Lecturer at the Manchester School of Art.

Michael Dean's practice foregrounds the idea of text as an interface between the artist's own experience and his audience's (displaced) experience of this in his work. His work takes the form of book works, posters and sculpture but keeps at its centre careful arrangements of evocative texts that suggest intimate fragments of lived experience. Dean both utilises the assumed 'directness' of text to communicate ideas and frustrates this through the use of existing and invented typefaces that serves to significantly slow the pace of the reader, delaying their absorption of the texts, or rendering the texts virtually unreadable. Dean was born in Newcastle-upon-Tyne, UK, in 1977 and studied Fine Art Practice and Contemporary Critical Theory at Goldsmiths College, London (1998 – 2001). He currently lives and works in London.

Sarah M. Harrison is an artist and writer. Her live performances, accompanied by video works, gently assault the senses, allowing audiences to experience unexpressed emotions of the subconscious for subliminal healing and organ balance. Most of her thought processes end in gore. She is interested in relational experiences of the abyss, the impossibility of going too far, the unbearable embarrassment of existing, and gossipy history.

Omar Kholeif is a writer, curator and editor. He has authored or edited nearly twenty books including, *You Are Here: Art After the Internet, Virgin with a Memory: The Exhibition Tie-In, Jeddah Childhood circa 1994, Before History* and *Two Days After Forever: A Reader on the Choreography of Time.*

Peter Kingstone is a Toronto-based visual artist and curator, working primarily in video and photography. As an independent artist, Peter's installation pieces have been shown across Canada and internationally, and he was awarded the Untitled Artist Award in 2005 for his installation *The Strange Case of Peter K.* (1974 – 2004). Peter holds a degree in Philosophy / Cultural Studies from Trent University in Peterborough and a Masters of Fine Art focussing on video and new media from York University in Toronto. Peter has presented at many conferences on ideas around storytelling and social engagement.

Claire Makhlouf Carter develops performance events and interventions, setting up an interruptive form which she terms 'organised gate-crashing' by juxtaposing a range of knowledge bases to explore relations critically. She often employs temporary workers drawing out the internalised and embodied complexities of social and institutional relations in order to simulate a critical institution. Recent performance events include *DEMO SKOYLES* (Eastside Projects, Birmingham, 2015); *DEMO DISTRACTION* (Learning Resource, TATE Modern, 2014); *DEMO KHAT* (DIG & Institutional Loser Symposium & Performance: Anthology Live, Camden Arts Centre, 2013–2014); *DEMO FABRIEK* (The Scene Changes to an Empty Room, De Fabriek, Eindhoven, Netherlands, 2012); *DEMO PENFOLD STREET* (Confrontational Perspectives, The Showroom Gallery London, 2012). Collaborative work includes *A Contract with a Heckler* performed at five conferences in 2013. Carter is a founding member of SPV Ltd. Her practice-based PhD at the RCA was awarded in 2012, entitled *Does She Stink?: How do you engage with work which rejects the complacency of shared experience and benign relationships; and how do you document the invisible worker, the antagonist or even the stink of your own fear?*

Laura Morrison's work in writing and gallery art examines the awkward clashes between what it means to be vulnerable and what it means to be accountable. Drawn from personal and professional networks, the stories and subjects that emerge from the work involve real-life gendered power struggles and often activate absurd tensions between the actual seriousness of painting and the inherent camp of self-promotion. Morrison graduated from the MFA at Goldsmiths. Her recent projects include *Magnetism* at Hazelwood House, Sligo; *Bottom Natures* at Cafe Gallery Projects, London; *The Conch* at The South London Gallery; *Vivian, Cape Town* at CANAL / Furnished Space, London; and *How To Read World Literature* at The Public School, New York. In 2014 she organised *Concerning The Bodyguard*, an exhibition and events programme at The Tetley, Leeds. Forthcoming projects include *Open Sessions* at The Drawing Center, New York; *Bain Marie* at Res., London; an online portfolio for *Bomb* magazine, New York; new writing in both *Wet Knickers* zine (UK) and for the *Word Processor* project at The Reanimation Library in New York.

Louise O'Hare is interested in the potentials of art publishing strategies. Ongoing projects include *Sonrisa*, a bilingual magazine of new work by artists based in Havana and London, and Three Letter Words, an organisation which is currently developing a new distribution channel for art publishers. In 2011 she founded the *London Bookshop Map*, a platform for disseminating text-based work by artists who have included Dora García, Katrina Palmer and Hannah Rickards among others. O'Hare is currently undertaking a PhD at Northumbria University (Funded Studentship Award, 2014–17) and is an associate editor at *Afterall*.

Bridget Penney was born in Edinburgh and now lives on the south coast of England. She is currently working on a novel and an assemblage of texts loosely centred around Abney Park Cemetery in North London that aims to explore how people construct narratives about place. A number of these have appeared online at *3:am* magazine and in print. In the 1990s she ran the small imprint Invisible Books with Paul Holman, publishing genre-defying poetry and prose. Her novel *Index* was published in Book Works' *Semina* series in 2008 and has recently been reprinted.

Sarah Perks is a curator, film producer and academic with significant experience of contemporary visual art and independent film. She is a specialist in artist feature film, performance and participatory art and has worked with international artists including Rosa Barba, Phil Collins, Rashid Rana and Stanya Kahn. In 2011, Sarah set up HOME Artist Film (then Cornerhouse Artist Film) as a means of investigating new methods for the production, distribution and exhibition of artist feature film. Her recent credits include co-curator of HOME's opening exhibition *The Heart is Deceitful Above All Things...* (May 2015) and *SAFE* (November 2015), the exhibition of which this publication is a part. Recent writing credits include a contribution to *Transactions of Desire: Volume 1* and AL & AL's *Incidents of Travel in the Multiverse* (forthcoming, February 2016). Sarah is also Professor of Visual Arts at Manchester School of Art, part of Manchester Metropolitan University.

Emma Jane Unsworth's first novel, *Hungry, the Stars and Everything* (Hidden Gem) won a Betty Trask Award from the Society of Authors and was shortlisted for the

Portico Prize in 2012. Her short story *I Arrive First* was included in *The Best British Short Stories 2012* (Salt). She has worked as a journalist, a columnist for *The Big Issue*, and a barmaid. Her second novel *Animals* was published by Canongate in May 2014. She is writing a third novel, as well as the screenplay of *Animals*, which has been optioned by BAFTA-nominated producer Sarah Brocklehurst and awarded development funding by the BFI.

John Walter (born 1978, Dartford) works in a range of media including drawing, painting, performance, video, music and sculpture. His installations are grounded in theoretical and empirical research, and they seduce visitors into engaging with complex and often uncomfortable subjects such as sexual health through his exuberant use of colour, humour and hospitality. Walter creates fictions that begin with his personal experience and quote the voices of others, weaving them together into new epic works. The term 'Maximalist', which best describes his work, refers to an additive practice that values the relationships between things rather than their qualities in isolation. Walter's work is visually intricate, returning to specific lexicons of imagery such as Tarot cards, which allow meanings to develop within multiple contexts. Recent exhibitions include *Courtship Disorder* (White Cubicle Toilet Gallery, 2015); *Alien Sex Club* (Ambika P3, 2015); and *Turn My Oyster Up* (Whitstable Biennale, 2014). He was awarded the Sainsbury Scholarship at the British School at Rome 2006–8 and was a participant in Skowhegan School of Painting and Sculpture in 2012.

Camilla Wills is an artist and editor currently based in Brussels.

Jason Wood is the Artistic Director of Film at HOME. He is the author of multiple books on cinema, most recently, *Last Words: Considering Contemporary Cinema* (Wallflower Press).

Transactions of Desire, Volume II:
Are You Allergic to the 21ST Century?
Edited by Louise O'Hare and Sarah Perks

First published in the United Kingdom in 2015 by:
HOME Publications

On the occasion of the exhibition:
SAFE
Saturday 14 November 2015 – Sunday 3 January 2016

HOME
2 Tony Wilson Place
First Street, Manchester
M15 4FN, United Kingdom
www.homemcr.org

ISBN: 978-0-9929524-5-7

AUTHORS
Hannah Black, Chris Paul Daniels, Michael Dean, Sarah M. Harrison, Omar Kholeif, Peter Kingstone, Claire Makhlouf Carter, Laura Morrison, Louise O'Hare, Bridget Penney, Sarah Perks, Emma Jane Unsworth, John Walter, Camilla Wills and Jason Wood.

EDITORS
Louise O'Hare and Sarah Perks

PRODUCER
Bren O'Callaghan

PROOFREADING
Greg Thorpe

DESIGN & ART DIRECTION
Minute Works

DISTRIBUTED WORLDWIDE BY
Cornerhouse Publications
www.cornerhousepublications.org

HOME

MANCHESTER
SCHOOL OF ART

TRANSACTIONS OF DESIRE, VOLUME II:
ARE YOU ALLERGIC TO THE 21ST CENTURY?